Sketches of the East Africa Campaign

Robert Valentine Dolbey

Contents

SKETCHES OF THE
EAST AFRICA CAMPAIGN

BY

Robert Valentine Dolbey

PREFACE

The bulk of these "Sketches" were written without any thought of publication. It was my practice in "writing home" to touch upon different features of the campaign or of my daily experiences, and only when I returned to England to find that kind hands had carefully preserved these hurried letters, did it occur to me that, grouped together, they might serve to throw some light on certain aspects of the East Africa campaign, which might not find a place in a more elaborate history.

For the illustrations, I have been able to draw upon a number of German photographs which fell into our hands.

I should like to take this opportunity of thanking Mr. H.T. Montague Bell for the care and kindness with which he has grouped this collection of inco-ordinate sketches and formed it into a more or less comprehensive whole.

ROBERT V. DOLBEY,
ITALY,
February, 1918.

INTRODUCTION

These sketches of General Smuts' campaign of 1916 in German East Africa, do not presume to give an accurate account of the tactical or strategical events of this war. The actual knowledge of the happenings of war and of the considerations that persuade an Army Commander to any course of military conduct must, of necessity, be a closed book to the individual soldier. To the fighting man himself and to the man on the lines of communication, who helps to feed and clothe and arm and doctor him, the history of his particular war is very meagre. War, to the soldier, is limited to the very narrow horizon of his front, the daily work of his regiment, or, at the most, of his brigade. Rarely does news from the rest of one brigade spread to the troops of another in the field. Only in the hospital that serves the division are the events of his bit of war correlated and reduced to a comprehensive whole. Even then the resulting knowledge is usually wrong. For the imagination of officers, and of men in particular, is wonderful, and rumour has its birthplace in the hospital ward. One may take it as an established fact that the ordinary regimental officer or soldier knows little or nothing about events other than his particular bit of country. Only the Staff know, and they will not tell. Sometimes we have thought that all the real news lives in the cloistered brain of the General and his Chief of Staff. Be this as it may, we always got fuller and better correlated and co-ordinated news of the German East African Campaign from "Reuter" or from *The Times* weekly edition.

But if the soldier in the forward division knows nothing of the strategical events of his war, there are many things of which he does know, and so well too that they eclipse the greater strategical considerations of the war. He does know the food he eats and the food that he would like to eat; moreover, he knew, in German East Africa, what his rations ought to be, and how to do without them. He learnt how to fight and march and carry heavy equipment on a very empty stomach. He learnt to eke out his meagre supplies by living on the wild game of the country, the native flour, bananas and mangoes. He knew what it meant to have dysentery and malaria. He had marched under a broiling sun by day and shivered in the tropic dews at night. He knew what it was to sleep upon the ground; to hunt for shade from the vertical sun. These and many other things did he know, and herein lies the chief interest of this or of any other campaign.

For, strange as it may seem, the soldier in East Africa was more concerned about his food and clothing, the tea he thirsted for, the blisters that tormented his weary feet, the equipment that was so heavy, the sleep that drugged his footsteps on the march, the lion that sniffed around his drowsy head at night, than about the actual fighting. These are the real points of personal interest in any campaign, and if these sketches bear upon the questions of food, the matter of transport, the manner of the soldier's illness, the hospitals he stayed in, the tsetse fly that bit him by day, the mosquitoes that made his nights a perfect torment, they are the more true to life. For fights are few, and, in this thick bush country, frequently degenerate into blind firing into a blinder bush; but the "jigger" flea is with the soldier always.

But this campaign is far different from any of the others in which our arms are at present engaged. First and of especial interest was this army of ours; the most heterogeneous collection of fighting men, from the ends of the earth, all gathered in one smoothly working homogeneous whole. From Boers and British South Africans, from Canada and Australia, from India, from home, from the planters of East Africa, and from all the dusky tribes of Central Africa, was this army of ours recruited. The country, too, was of such a character that knowledge of war in other campaigns was of little value. Thick grass, dense thorn scrub, high elephant grass, all had their special bearing on the quality of the fighting. Close-quarter engagements were the rule, dirty fighting in the jungle, ambushes, patrol encounters; and the deadly machine-gun that enfiladed or swept every open space. We cannot be surprised that the mounted arm was robbed of much of its utility, that artillery work was often blind for want of observation, that the trench dug in the green heart of a forest escaped the watchful eyes of aeroplanes, that this war became a fight of men and rifles, and, above all, the machine-gun.

In this campaign the Hun has been the least of the malignant influences. More from fever and dysentery, from biting flies, from ticks and crawling beasts have we suffered than from the bullets of the enemy. Lions and hyaenas have been our camp followers, and not a little are we grateful to these wonderful scavengers, the best of all possible allies in settling the great question of sanitation in camps. For all our roads were marked by the bodies of dead horses, mules and oxen, whose stench filled the evening air. Much labour in the distasteful jobs of burying these poor victims of war did the scavengers of the forest save us.

The transport suffered from three great scourges: the pest of horse-sickness and fly and the calamity of rain. For after twelve hours' rain in that black cotton soil never a wheel could move until a hot sun had dried the surface of the roads again. Roads, too, were mere bush tracks in the forest, knee-deep either in dust or in greasy clinging mud.

Never has Napoleon's maxim that "an army fights on its stomach" been better exemplified than here. All this campaign we have marched away from our dinners, as the Hun has marched toward his. The line of retreat, predetermined by the enemy, placed him in the fortunate position that the further he marched the more food he got, the softer bed, more ammunition, and the moral comfort of his big naval guns that he fought to a standstill and then abandoned. Heavy artillery meant hundreds of native porters or dove-coloured humped oxen of the country to drag them; and heavy roads defied the most powerful machinery to move the guns.

In order to appreciate the great difficulty with which our Supply Department has had to contend, we must remember that our lines of communication have been among the longest in any campaign. From the point of view of the railway and the road haul of supplies, our lines of communication have been longer than those in the Russo-Japanese War. For every pound of bully beef or biscuit or box of ammunition has been landed at Kilindini, our sea base, from England or Australia, railed up to Voi or Nairobi, a journey roughly of 300 miles. From one or other of those distributing points the trucks have had to be dragged to Moschi on the German railway, from there eastward along the German railway line to Tanga as far as Korogwe, a matter of another 500 miles. From here the last stage of 200 miles has been covered by ox or mule or horse transport, and the all-conquering motor lorry, over these bush tracks to Morogoro. Can we wonder, then, that the great object of this campaign has been to raise as many supplies locally as possible, and to drive our beef upon the hoof in the rear of our advancing army? Nor is the German unconscious of these our difficulties. He has with the greatest care denuded the whole country of supplies before us, and called in to his aid his two great allies, the tsetse fly and horse sickness, to rob us of our live cattle and transport animals on the way.

At first we thought the German in East Africa to be a better fellow than his brother in Europe, more merciful to his wounded prisoner, more chivalrous in his manner of fighting. But the more we learn of him the more we come to the conclusion that he is the same old Hun as he is in Belgium--infinitely crafty, incredibly beastly in his dealings with his natives and with our prisoners. Only in one aspect did we find him different, and this by reason of the fact that we were winning and advancing, taking his plantations and his farms, finding that he had left his women and children to our charge. Then we saw the alteration. For I had known what eight months in German prisons in Europe mean to a soldier prisoner of war, and now I had German prisoners in my charge. Anxious to please, eager to conciliate, as infinitely servile to us, now they were in captivity, as they were vile and bestial and arrogant to us when they were in authority, were these prisoners of ours.

Nor was this the only aspect from which the campaign in German East Africa appealed to those of us who had taken part in the advance from the Marne to the Aisne in September, 1914. Then we saw what looting meant, and how the German officer enriched his family home with trophies looted from many chateaux. We knew of French houses that had been stripped of every article of value; we saw, discarded by the roadside, in the rapid and disorganised retreat to the Aisne, statuary and bronzes, pictures and clocks, and all the treasures of French homes. Now we were in a position to loot; but how differently our officers and men behaved! The spoils of hundreds of German plantations at our mercy; and hardly a thing, save what was urgently needed for hospitals or food, taken. Every house in which the German owner lived was left unmolested; only those abandoned to the mercy of the native plunderer had we entered. It pays a great tribute to the natural goodness of our men, that the German example of indiscriminate looting and destruction was not followed.

To people in England, and, indeed, to many soldiers in France, it seemed that this campaign of ours in German East Africa was a mere side-show. It appeared to be a Heaven-sent opportunity to escape the cold wet misery of the trenches in

Flanders. To some it spelt an expedition of the picnic variety; they saw in this an opportunity of spending halcyon days in the game preserves, glorious opportunities for making collections of big game heads, all sandwiched in with pleasant and successful enterprises against an enemy that was waiting only a decent excuse to surrender.

How different has been the reality, however! The picnic enterprise has turned out to be one of the most arduous in our experience. Many of us had served in France and the Dardanelles before, and we thought we knew what the hardships of war could mean. If the truth be told, the soldier suffered in East Africa, in many ways, greater hardships, performed greater feats of endurance, endured more from fever and dysentery and the many plagues of the country than in either of the other campaigns; the soldier marched and fought and suffered and starved for the simple reason that time was of the essence of the whole campaign. From June until Christmas we had to crowd in the campaigning of a whole year; for once the rains had started all fighting was perforce at an end. Once the transport wheels had stopped in the black cotton soil mud the army had to halt. All the time the great aim of the expedition was to get on and farther on. We had to advance and risk the shortage of supplies, or we would never reach the Central Railway. And there was not a soldier who would not prefer to push on and suffer and finish the campaign than wait in elegant leisure with full rations to contemplate an endless war in the swamps of East Africa.

The early history of the war in this theatre had been far from favourable to our arms. In late 1914 our Expeditionary Force failed in their landing at Tanga, a misfortune that was not compensated for by our subsequent reverse at Jassin near the Anglo-German border on the coast. The gallant though unsuccessful defence of the latter town by our Indian troops, however, caused great losses to the enemy, and robbed him of many of his most distinguished officers. But against these we must record the very fine defence of the Uganda Railway and the successful affair at Longido near the great Magadi Soda Lake in the Kilimanjaro area. But when South Africa, in 1916, was called in to redress the balance of India in German East Africa, the new strategic railway from Voi to the German frontier was only just commenced, and the enemy were in occupation of our territory at Taveta. To General Smuts then fell the task of co-ordinating the various units in British East Africa, strengthening them with South African troops, pushing on the railway toward Moschi, and driving the German from British soil. In so far as his initial movements were concerned, General Smuts carried out the plans evolved by his predecessors. After a series of difficult but brilliant engagements, the enemy were forced back to Moschi, and to the Kilimanjaro area, which, in places, was very strongly held. From this point he mapped out his own campaign. Colonel von Lettow was out-ma-noeuvred by our flanking movements, and forced to retire partly along the Tanga railway eastward to the sea, and partly towards the Central Railway in the heart of the enemy country.

Two outstanding features of this campaign may be mentioned: the faith the whole army had in General Smuts, the loyalty, absolute and complete, that all our heterogeneous troops gave to him; and the natural goodness of the soldier. As for the latter, Boer or English, Canadian, East African or Indian, all showed that they could bear the heat and dust and dirty fighting, the disease and privation just as gallantly, uncomplainingly, and well, as did their British comrades on the Western front.

Finally, there is one very generous tribute that our army would pay to the Germans in the field, and that is to the excellence of the leadership of Lettow, and the devotion with which he has by threats and cajolings sustained the failing courage of his men. Nor can one forget that in this war the mainstay of our enemy has lain in the discipline and devotion of the native troops. Here, indeed, in this campaign the black man has kept up the spirit of the white. Nor does this leave the future unclouded with potential trouble, for, in this war, the black man has seen the white, on both sides, run from him. The black man is armed and trained in the use of the rifle, and machine-gun, and his intelligence and capacity have been attested to by the degree of fire control that he mastered. It must be more than a coincidence that in the two colonies--East Africa and the Cameroon--where the Germans used native troops they put up an efficient and skilful resistance, while in South-West Africa, where all the enemy troops were white, they showed little inclination for a fight to a finish. In Colonel von Lettow-Vorbeck the German army has one of the most able and resourceful leaders that it has produced in this war.

THIS ARMY OF OURS

Since Alexander of Macedon descended upon the plains of India, there can never have been so strange and heterogeneous an army as this, and a doctor must speak with the tongues of men and angels to arrive at an even approximate understanding of their varied ailments. The first division that came with Jan Smuts from the snows of Kilimanjaro to the torrid delta of the Rufigi contained them all.

The real history of the war begins with Smuts; for, prior to his coming, we were merely at war; but when he came we began to fight. A brief twenty-four hours in Nairobi, during which he avoided the public receptions and the dinners that a more social chief would have graced; then he was off into the bush. Wherever that rather short, but well-knit figure appeared, with his red beard, well streaked with grey, beneath the red Staff cap, confidence reigned in all our troops. And to the end this trust has remained unabated. Many disappointments have come his way, more from his own mounted troops than from any others; but we have felt that his tactics and strategy were never wrong. Thus it was that from this heterogeneous army, Imperial, East African, Indian and South African, he has had a loyalty most splendid all the time. He may have pushed us forward so that we marched far in advance of food or supplies, thrust us into advanced positions that to our military sense seemed very hazardous. But he meant "getting a move on," and we knew it; and all of us wished the war to be over. Jan Smuts suffered the same fever as we did, ate our food, and his personal courage in private and most risky reconnaissances filled us with admiration and fear, lest disaster from some German patrol might overtake him. To me the absence of criticism and the loyal co-operation of all troops have been most wonderful. For we are an incurably critical people, and here was a civilian, come to wrest victory from a series of disasters.

First in interest, perhaps, as they were ever first in fight, are the Rhodesians, those careless, graceful fellows that have been here a year before the big advance began. Straight from the bush country and fever of Northern Rhodesia, they were probably the best equipped of all white troops to meet the vicissitudes of this warfare. They knew the dangers of the native paths that wound their way through the thorn bush, and gave such opportunities for ambush to the lurking patrol. None knew as they how to avoid the inviting open space giving so good a field of fire for the machine-gun, that took such toll of all our enterprises. With them, too, they brought a liability to blackwater fever that laid them low, a legacy from Lake Nyasa that marked them out as the victims of this scourge in the first year of the big advance.

The Loyal North Lancashires, too, have borne the heat and burden of the day from the first disastrous landing at Tanga. Always exceedingly well disciplined, they yield to none in the amount of solid unrewarded work done in this campaign.

Of the most romantic interest probably are the 25th Royal Fusiliers, the Legion of Frontiersmen. Volumes might be written of the varied careers and wild lives lived by these strange soldiers of fortune. They were led by Colonel Driscoll, who, for all his sixty years, has found no work too arduous and no climate too unhealthy for his brave spirit. I knew him in the Boer War when he commanded Driscoll's Scouts, of happy, though irregular memory; their badge in those days, the harp of Erin on the side of their slouch hats, and known throughout the country wherever there was fighting to be had. The 25th Fusiliers, too, were out here in the early days, and participated in the capture of Bukoba on the Lake. A hundred professions are represented in their ranks. Miners from Australia and the Congo, prospectors after the precious mineral earths of Siam and the Malay States, pearl-fishers and elephant poachers, actors and opera singers, jugglers, professional strong men, big-game hunters, sailors, all mingled with professions of peace, medicine, the law and the clerk's varied trade. Here two Englishmen, soldiers of fortune or misfortune, as the case might be, who had specialised in recent Mexican revolutions, till the fall of Huerta brought them, too, to unemployment; an Irishman there, for whom the President of Costa Rica had promised a swift death against a blank wall. Cunning in the art of gun-running, they were knowing in all the tides of the Caribbean Sea, and in every dodge to outwit the United States patrol. Nor must I forget one priceless fellow, a lion-tamer, who, strange to say, feared exceedingly the wild denizens of the scrub that sniffed around his patrol at night.

Of our Indian forces the most likeable and attractive were the Kashmiris, whom the patriot Rajah of Kashmir has given to the India Government. Recruited from the mountains of Nepal--for the native of Kashmir is no soldier--they meet one everywhere with their eager smiling faces. In hospital they are always professing to a recovery from fever that their pallid faces and enlarged spleens belie, and they take not kindly to any suggestion of invaliding.

These battalions of Kashmir Rifles, the Baluchis and the King's African Rifles have done more dirty bush fighting than any troops in this campaign. The Baluchis, in particular, have covered themselves with glory in many a fight.

The most efficient soldiers in East Africa are the King's African Rifles; unaffected by the fever and the dysentery of the country, and led by picked white officers, they are in their element in the thorn jungle in which the Germans have conducted their rearguard actions. Known at first as the "Suicides Club," the King's African Rifles lost a far greater proportion of officers than any other regiment. Nor is it a little that they owe to the gallant leader of one battalion, Colonel Graham, who lost his life early in the advance on Moschi. These regiments are recruited from Nyasaland in the south to Nubia and Abyssinia in the north. Yaos, known by the three vertical slits in their cheeks; slim Nandi, with perforated lobes to their ears; ebony Kavirondo; Sudanese of an excellent quality; Wanyamwezi from the country between Tabora and Lake Tanganyika, the very tribe from whom the German Askaris are recruited, and all the dusky tribes that stretch far north to Lake Rudolph and the Nile. Nor should one forget the Arab Rifles, raised by that wonderful fellow Wavell, whose brother was a prisoner with me in Germany. A professing Mohammedan, he was one of very few white men who had made the pilgrimage to Mecca. He harried the Huns along the unhealthy districts of the coast, until a patrol, in ambush, laid him low near Gazi.

Last, and most important, the army of South Africans, whose coming spelt for us the big advance and the swift move that made us master of the whole country from Kilimanjaro to the Rufigi. A great political experiment and a most wonderfully successful one was this Africander army, English and Boers, under a Boer General. For the first time since the Great War in South Africa, the Boers made common cause with us, definitely aligned themselves with us in a joint campaign and provided the greatest object lesson of this World War. If the campaign of German East Africa was worth while, its value has been abundantly proved in this welding of the races that, despite local disagreements, has occurred. The South African troops have found the country ill adapted to their peculiar genius in war, and the blind bush has robbed the mounted arm of much of its efficiency. Not here the wide distances to favour their enveloping tactics. Much have they suffered from fever, hardships and privation, and to their credit lies the greatest of all marches in this campaign, the 250 mile march to Kondoa Irangi in the height of the rainy season. The South African Infantry arrived in Kondoa starved and worn and bootless after this forced march to extricate the mounted troops, whose impetuous ardour had thrust them far beyond the possibility of supplies, into the heart of the enemy's country. We cannot sufficiently praise the apparently reckless tactics that made this wonderful march towards the Central Railway, or the uncomplaining fortitude of troops who lived in this fever-stricken country, on hippopotamus meat, wild game and native meal. To the Boer, as to all of us, this campaign must have taught a wonderful lesson, for many prejudices have been modified, and it has been learnt that "coolies" (as only too often the ignorant style all natives of India) and "Kaffirs," can fight with the best.

This campaign would have been largely impossible, were it not for the Cape Boys and other natives from the Union, who have come to run our mule and ox transport. Their peculiar genius is the management of horses, mules and cattle. Different from other primitive and negro people, they are very kind to animals, infinitely knowledgeable in the lore of mule and ox, they can be depended upon to exact the most from animal transport with the least cruelty. Wonderful riders these; I have seen them sit bucking horses in a way that a Texas cowboy or a Mexican might envy.

One should not leave the subject of this army without reference to the Cape Corps--that experiment in military recruiting which many of us were at first inclined to condemn. But from the moment the Cape Boy enlisted in the ranks of the Cape Corps his status was raised, and he adopted, together with his regulation khaki uniform and helmet, a higher responsibility towards the army than did his brother who helped to run the transport. They have been well officered, they have been a lesson to all of us in the essential matters of discipline and smartness, they have done much of the dirty work entailed by guarding lines of communication, and now, when given their longed-for chance of actual fighting on the Rufigi, they have covered themselves with distinction. For my part, as a doctor, I found they had too much ego in their cosmos, as is commonly the fault of half-bred races, and a sick Cape Corps soldier seemed always very sick indeed; yet, as the campaign progressed, we came to like and to admire these troops the more, so that their distinction won in the Rufigi fighting was welcomed very gladly by all of us.

Later in the campaign arrived the Gold Coast Regiment; and now the Nigerian Brigade are here. Very, very smart and soldier-like these Hausa and Fulani troops; Mohammedan, largely, in religion, and bearded where the East Coast native is smooth-faced, they will stay to finish this guerilla fighting, for which their experience in the Cameroon has so well fitted them. The Gold Coast Regiment has always been where there has been the hardest fighting, their green woollen caps and leather sandals marking them out from other negroid soldiers. And their impetuous courage has won them many captured enemy guns, and, alas! a very long list of casualties. But in hospital they are the merriest of happy people, always joking and smiling, and are quite a contrast to our much more serious East Coast native; they have earned from their white sergeants and officers very great admiration and devotion. By far the best equipped of any unit in the field, they had, as a regiment, no less than eight machine-guns and a regimental mountain battery.

THE NAVY AND ITS WORK

To the Navy that alone has made this campaign possible, we soldiers owe our grateful thanks. But there have been times when, in our blindness, we have failed to realise how great the task was to blockade 400 miles of this coast and to keep a watchful eye on Mozambique. For before the Portuguese made common cause with us, there was a great deal of gun-running along the southern border of German East Africa, which our present Allies found impossible to watch. Two factors materially aided the Germans in making the fight they have. First, there was the lucky "coincidence" of the Dar-es-Salaam Exhibition. This exhibition, which was to bring the whole world to German East Africa in August, 1914, provided the military authorities with great supplies of machinery, stores and exhibits from all the big industrial centres; and these were swiftly adapted to the making of rifles and munitions of war. To this must be added the most important factor of all, the *Koenigsberg*, lying on the mud flats far up the Rufigi, destroyed by us, it is true, but not before the ship's company of 700, officers and men, and most of the guns had been transported ashore, the latter mounted on gun carriages and dragged by weary oxen or thousands of black porters to dispute our advance. In due course, however, these were abandoned, one by one, as we pressed the enemy back from the Northern Railway south to the Rufigi. Last, but by no means least, was the moral support their wireless stations gave them. These, though unable, since the destruction of the main stations, to transmit messages, continued for some time to receive the news from Nauen in Germany. By the air from Germany the officers received the Iron Cross, promotion, and the Emperor's grateful thanks.

But if you would see what work the Navy has done, you must first begin at Lindi in the south. There you will see the *Praesident* of the D.O.A. line lying on her side with her propellers blown off and waiting for our tugs to drag her to Durban for repair. And in the Rufigi lying on the mudbanks, fourteen miles from the mouth, you will see the *Koenigsberg*, once the pride of German cruisers, half sunk and completely dismantled. The hippopotami scratch their tick-infested flanks upon her rusted sides, crocodiles crawl across her decks, fish swim through the open ports. In Dar-es-Salaam you will see the *Koenig* stranded at the harbour mouth, the *Tabora* lying on her side behind the ineffectual shelter of the land; the side uppermost innocent of the Red Cross and green line that adorned her seaward side. For she was a mysterious craft. She flew the Red Cross and was tricked out as a hospital ship on one side, the other painted grey. True, she had patients and a doctor on board when a pinnace from one of our cruisers examined her, but she also had machine-guns mounted and gun emplacements screwed to her deck, and all the adaptations required for a commerce raider. So our admiral decided that, after due notice, so suspicious a craft were better sunk. A few shots flooded her compartments and she heeled over, burying the lying Cross of Geneva beneath the waters of the harbour. Further up the creek you will see the *Feldmarschall* afloat and uninjured, save for the engines that our naval party had destroyed, and ready, to our amazement, at the capture of the town, to be towed to Durban and to carry British freight to British ports, and maybe meet a destroying German submarine upon the way. Further up still you will find the Governor's yacht and a gunboat, sunk this time by the Germans; but easy to raise and to adapt for our service. Strange that so methodical a people should have bungled so badly the simple task of rendering a valuable ship useless for the enemy. But they have blundered in the execution of their plans everywhere. The attempt to obstruct the harbour mouth at Dar-es-Salaam was typical of their naval ineptitude. Barely two hundred yards across this bottle-neck, it should have been an easy job to block. So they sank the floating dock in the southern portion of the channel and moored the *Koenig* by bow and stern hawsers, to the shores on either side in position for sinking. Instead of flooding her they prepared an explosive bomb and timed it to go off at the fall of the tide. But the bomb failed to explode, and an ebb tide setting in, broke the stern moorings and drove her sideways on the shore. Here she lies now and the channel is still free to all our ships to come and go. We found, at the occupation, the record of the court-martial on the German naval officer responsible for the failure of the plan. He seems to have pleaded, with success, the fact that his dynamite was fifteen years old. After that no further attempt was made, and for nearly a year before we occupied the town our naval whalers and small cruisers sailed, the white ensign proudly flying, into the harbour to anchor and to watch the interned shipping. It must have been a humiliating spectacle to the Hun; but he was helpless. Woe betide him, if he placed a mine or trained a gun upon this ship of ours. The town would have suffered, and this they could not risk.

Yet further up the coast, near Tanga, the *Markgraf* lies beached in shallow water, and the *Reubens* a wreck in Mansa Bay.

In most of our naval operations our intelligence has been excellent, and Fortune has been kind. It seemed to the Germans that we employed some special witchcraft to provide the knowledge that we possessed. So they panicked ingloriously, and sought spies everywhere, and hanged inoffensive natives by the dozen to the mango trees. One day one of our whalers entered Tanga harbour the very day the German mines were lifted for the periodical overhaul. The Germans ascribed such knowledge to the Prince of Evil. The whaler proceeded to destroy a ship lying there, and, on its way out, fired a shell into a lighter that was lying near. In this lighter were the mines, as the resulting explosion testified. This completed the German belief in our possession of supernatural powers of obtaining information.

Again at the bombardment and capture of Bagamoyo by the Fleet, it seemed to the Hun that wherever the German commander went, to this trench or to that observation post, our 6-inch shells would follow him. All day long they pursued his footsteps, till he also panicked and searched the bush for a hidden wireless. He it was who shot our gallant Marine officer, as our men stormed the trenches, and paid the penalty for his rashness shortly after.

The little German tug *Adjutant*, which in times of peace plied across the bar at Chinde to bring off passengers and mails to the ships that lay outside, has had a chequered career in this war. Slipping out from Chinde at the outbreak of war, she made her way to Dar-es-Salaam. From there she essayed another escapade only to fall into our hands. Transformed into a gunboat, she harried the Germans in the Delta of the Rufigi, until, greatly daring, one day she ran ashore on a mudbank in the river. Captured with her crew she was taken to pieces by the Germans and transported by rail to Ujiji on Lake Tanganyika. And there the Belgians found her, partly reconstructed, as they entered the harbour. A little longer delay, and the resurrected *Adjutant* would have played havoc with our small craft and the Belgians', which had driven the German ships off the vast waters of this lake.

LETTOW AND HIS ARMY

Lettow, the one-eyed, or to give him his full title, Colonel von Lettow-Vorbeck, is the heart and soul of the German resistance in East Africa. Indomitable and ubiquitous, he has kept up the drooping spirits of his men by encouragement, by the example of great personal courage, and by threats that he can and will carry out. Wounded three times, he has never left his army, but has been carried about on a "machela" to prevent the half-resistance that leads to surrender. And now we hear he has had blackwater, and, recovering, has resumed his elusive journeys from one discouraged company to another all over the narrowing area of operations that alone is left to the Hun of his favourite colonial possessions. For to the fat shipping clerk of Tanga, whose soul lives only for beer and the leave that comes to reward two years of effort, the temptation to go sick or to get lost in the bush in front of our advancing armies is very great. He is not of the stuff that heroes are made of, and surrender is so safe and easy. A prison camp in Bombay is clearly preferable to this unending retreat. He has done enough for honour, he argues, he has proved his worth after two and a half years of resistance! This colony has put up the best fight of all, "and the *Schwein Englaender* holds the seas, so further resistance is hopeless." "We are not barbarians, are we Fritz?" But Fritz has ceased to care. "Ahmednagar for mine," says he, reverting to the language he learnt in the brewery at Milwaukee, in days that now seem to belong to some antenatal life. Soon he will look for some white face beneath the strange sun helmet the English wear, up will go his hands, and "Kamerad"--that magic word--will open the doors to sumptuous ease behind the prison bars.

But Lettow is going "all out." His black Askaris are not discouraged, and, in this war, the black man is keeping up the courage of the white. Had the native soldiers got their tails down the game was up as far as the Germans were concerned. But these faithful fellows see the "Bwona Kuba," as they call Lettow, here encouraging, everywhere inspiring them by his example, and they will stay with him until the end. Like many great soldiers, Lettow is singularly careless in his dress; and the tale is told at Moschi of a young German officer who stole a day's leave and discussed with a stranger at a shop window the chances of the ubiquitous Lettow arriving to spoil his afternoon. Nor did he know until he found the reprimand awaiting him in camp that he had been discussing the ethics of breaking out of camp with the "terror" himself.

A soldier of fortune is Lettow. His name is stained with the hideous massacres of the Hereros in South-West Africa. His was the order, transmitted through the German Governor's mouth, that thrust the Herero women and children into the deserts of Damaraland to die. Before the war in South Africa, rumour says, he was instructor to the "Staats Artillerie," which Kruger raised to stay the storm that he knew inevitably would overwhelm him. Serving, with Smuts and Botha themselves in the early months of the Boer war, he joined the inglorious procession of foreigners that fled across the bridge at Komati Poort after Pretoria fell, and left the Boer to fight it out unaided for two long and weary years more. No wonder that Lettow has sworn never to surrender to that "damned Dutchman Jan Smuts." Chary of giving praise for work well done, he yet is inexorable to failure. The tale is told that Lettow was furious when Fischer, the major in command at Moschi, was bluffed out of his impregnable position there by Vandeventer, evacuated the northern lines, and retired on Kahe, thus saving us the expense of taking a natural fortress that would have taxed all our energies. White with rage, he sent for Fischer and handed him one of his own revolvers. "Let me hear some interesting news about you in a day or two." And Fischer took the pistol and walked away to consider his death warrant. He looked at that grim message for two days before he could summon up his courage: then he shot himself, well below the heart, in a spot that he thought was fairly safe. But poor Fischer's knowledge of anatomy was as unsound as his strategy, for the bullet perforated his stomach. And it took him three days to die.

A tribe which has contributed largely to the German military forces is the Wanyamwezi. Of excellent physique, they long resisted German domination, but now they are entirely subdued. Hardy, brave and willing, they are the best fighters and porters, probably, in the whole of East Africa. Immigrant Wanyamwezi, enlisted in British East Africa into our King's African Rifles, do not hesitate to fight against their blood brothers. There is no stint to the faithful service they have given to the Germans. But for them our task would have been much easier. For drilling and parade the native mind shows great keenness and aptitude; little squads of men are drilled voluntarily by their own N.C.O.'s in their spare time; and often, just after an official drill is over, they drill one another again. Smart and well-disciplined they are most punctilious in all military services.

INTELLIGENCE

Of all the departments of War in German East Africa probably the most romantic and interesting is the Intelligence Department. Far away ahead of the fighting troops are the Intelligence officers with their native scouts. These officers, for the most part, are men who have lived long in the country, who know the native languages, and are familiar with the lie of the land from experience gained in past hunting trips. Often behind the enemy, creeping along the lines of communication, these officers carry their lives in their hands, and run the risk of betrayal by any native who happens across them. Sleeping in the bush at night, unable to light fires to cook their food, lest the light should attract the questing patrol, that, learning of their presence in the country, has been out after them for days. Hiding in the bush, short of rations, the little luxuries of civilisation long since finished, forced to smoke the reeking pungent native tobacco, living off wild game (that must be trapped, not shot), and native meal, at the mercy of the natives whom both sides employ to get information of the other, these men are in constant danger. Nor are the amenities of civilised warfare theirs when capture is their lot.

Fortunately for the British Empire there has never been any lack of those restless beings whose wandering spirits lead them to the confines of civilisation and beyond. To this type of man the African continent has offered a particular attraction, and we should have fared badly in the East African campaign, if we could not have relied upon the services of many of them. They are for the most part men who have abandoned at an early age the prosaic existence previously mapped out for them, and plunging into the wilds of Africa have found a more attractive livelihood in big game shooting and prospecting. By far the most exhilarating calling is that of the elephant hunter, who finds in the profits he derives from it all the compensation he requires for the hardships, the long marches, and the grave personal dangers. In the most inaccessible parts of the continent he plies his trade, knowing that his life may depend upon the quickness of his eye and intellect and the accuracy of his aim. Nor are his troubles over when his quarry has been secured. The ivory has still to be disposed of, and it is not always safe to attempt to sell in the territory where the game has been shot. The area of no man's land in Africa has long since been a diminishing quantity, and the promiscuous shooting of elephants is not encouraged. It becomes necessary, therefore, to study the question of markets, and the successful hunter finds it convenient to vary the spheres of his activities continually.

Not the least of the assets of these men is the knowledge they have of the native and the hold they have obtained over them. That man will go farthest who relies on the respect rather than on the fear he inspires. The latter may go a long way, but unless it has the former to support it, the chances are against it sooner or later. One man I know of owed his life more than once to his devotion to a small stick that walking, sitting or lying he never allowed out of his hand. The native mind came to attach magical powers to the stick, and consequently to the man himself. On one eventful journey when he had gone farther afield than his wont, and farther than his native porters cared to accompany him, symptoms of mutiny made their appearance. A council was held as to whether he should be murdered or not; he was fortunate enough to overhear it. The only possible deterrent seemed to be a dread of the magical stick, but the two ringleaders affected to make light of it. Realising that the time had come for decisive action, the white man summoned the company, told them that his stick had revealed the plot to him and warned them of the danger they ran. To clinch his argument he offered to allow the ringleaders to return home, taking the stick with them; but told them that they would be dead within twenty-four hours, and the stick would come back to him. To his dismay they accepted the challenge, and for him there could be no retreat. In desperation he poisoned the food they were to take with them, and awaited developments. The two natives set off early in the morning. By the afternoon they were back again, and with them the stick. In the solitude of their homeward trek their courage had oozed out; they feared the magic, and fortunately had not touched the poisoned provisions. In the feasting that had to celebrate this satisfactory denouement it was possible to substitute other food for that which had been taken on the abortive journey. Magic or the fear of it had saved the situation; but the instincts of loyalty had been fired previously by a character that had many attractive features and never allowed firmness to dispossess justice.

At the outbreak of the war two of our Nimrods--whom I shall call Hallam and Best--were camped by the Rovuma river. Hearing that there were British ships at Lindi, they made for the coast to offer their services in the sterner hunt, after much more dangerous game, that they knew had now begun. The native runner that brought them the news from Mozambique also warned them of the German force that was hot foot in pursuit of them. So they tarried not in the order of their going, and made for the shelter of the fleet. But Best would read his weekly *Times* by the light of the lamp at their camp table for all the Huns in Christendom, he said, and derided Hallam's surer sense of danger near at hand. So in the early hours their pickets came running in, all mixed up with German Askaris, and the ring of rifle and machine-gun fire told them that their time had come. Capsizing the tell-tale lamp, they scattered in the undergrowth like a covey of partridges, Hallam badly wounded in the leg and only able to crawl. The friendly shelter of the papyrus leaves beside the river-bank was his refuge; and as he plunged into the river the scattered volley of rifle shots tore the reeds above him. All night they remained there. Hallam up to his neck in water, and the ready prey of any searching crocodile that the blood that oozed from his wounded leg should inevitably have attracted; the Germans on the bank. Next morning the trail of blood towards the river assured the enemy that Hallam was no more, for who could live in these dangerous waters all night, wounded as he was? But if Hallam could hunt like a leopard, he could also swim like a fish. Next day brought a native fishing canoe into sight, and to it he swam, still clutching the rifle that second nature had caused him to grab as he plunged into the reeds. With a wet rifle and nine cartridges he persuaded the natives not only to ferry him across to the Portuguese side, but also to carry him in a "machela," a hammock slung between native porters, from which he shot "impala" for his food. But somehow word had got across the river that Hallam had eluded death, and the German Governor stormed and threatened till the Portuguese sent police to arrest the fugitive. But the native runner who brought him news of his discovery also brought word of the approaching police. So with his rifle and three cartridges to sustain him, often delirious with fever, and the inflammation in his leg, he commandeered the men of a native village and persuaded them, such was the prestige of his name, to carry him twenty-eight days in the "machela" to a friendly mission station on Lake Nyasa. Here the kindly English sisters nursed him back to life and health again.

Best was not so lucky, for he was taken prisoner. But there was no German gaol that could hold so resourceful a prisoner as this. In due time he made his escape, and was to be found later looping the loop above Turkish camps in the Sinai Peninsula.

One German, of whom our information had been that "his company did little else but rape women and loot goats," fell into my hands when we took the English Universities Mission at Korogwe. Could this be he, I thought, as I saw an officer of mild appearance and benevolent aspect speaking English so perfectly and peering at me through big spectacles? Badly wounded and with a fracture of the thigh, he had begged me to look after him, saying the most disloyal things about the character and surgical capacity of the German doctor whom we had left behind to look after German wounded. Not that the *Oberstabsarzt* did not deserve them, but it was so gratuitously beastly to say them to me, an enemy. He deplored, too, with such unctuous phrases, the fact that war should ever have occurred in East Africa. How it would spoil the years of toil, toward Christianity, of many mission stations! How the simple native had been taught in this war to kill white men; hitherto, of course, the vilest of crimes. How the march of civilisation had been put back for twenty-five years. How the prestige of the white man had fallen, for had not natives seen white men, on both sides, run away before them? Many such pious expressions issued from his lips. But the true Hun character came out when he asked whether the hated Boers were coming? The most vindictive expression, that even the benevolent spectacles could only partly modify, clouded his face, and he complained to me most bitterly of the black ingratitude of the Boers toward Germany. "All my life, from boyhood," he complained, "have I not subscribed my pfennigs to provide Christmas presents for the poor Boers suffering under the heel of England. Did not German girls," he whined, "knit stockings for the women of that nation that was so akin to the Germans in blood, and that lay so pitifully prostrate beneath the feet of England?" Nor would he be appeased until I assured him that the Boers were far away.

Another, whose reputation was that of "a hard case, and addicted to drink," I found also in hospital in Korogwe, recovered from an operation for abscess of the liver, and living in hospital with his wife. Spruce and rather jumpy he insisted on exhibiting his operation wound to me, paying heavy compliments to English skill in surgery; not, mark you, that he had any but the greatest contempt that all German doctors, too, profess for British medicine and surgery. But he hoped, by specious praise, to be sent to Wilhelmstal and not to join the other prisoners in Ahmednagar. Bottles of soda-water ostentatiously displayed upon his table might have suggested what his bleary eye and shaky hands belied. So I contented myself with removing the pass key to the wine cellar, that lay upon the sideboard, and duly marked him down on the list for transfer to Wilhelmstal.

That the spirit of Baron Munchausen still lives in German East Africa is attested to by Intelligence reports. It says a great deal for Lettow's belief in the accuracy of our information that he very promptly put a stop to the notoriety and reputation for valour that two German officers enjoyed. One had made an unsuccessful attempt to bomb the Uganda Railway on two occasions; but neither time did he do any damage, though, on each occasion, he claimed to have cut the line. The other, possessed of greater imagination, reported to his German commander that he had attacked one of our posts along the railway, completely destroying it and all in it. The painful truth he learnt afterwards from German headquarters was that the English suffered no casualties, and the post was comparatively undamaged.

The sad fate of one enterprising German officer who set out to make an attack upon one of our posts was, at the time, the cause, of endless jesting at the expense of the Survey and Topographical Department of British East Africa. He was relying upon an old English map of the country, but owing to its extreme inaccuracy, he lost his way, ran out of water, and made an inglorious surrender. This, of course, was attributed by the Germans to the low cunning employed by our Intelligence Department that allowed the German authorities to get possession of a misleading map.

That retribution follows in the wake of an unpopular German officer, as shown by extracts from captured German diaries, is attested to by the record of two grim tragedies in the African bush, one of an officer who "lost his way," the other of an officer who was shot by his own men.

GERMAN TREATMENT OF NATIVES

One of the features of German military life that fills one with horror and disgust is their brutality to the native. Nor do they make any attempt to cloak their atrocities. For they perpetuate them by photographs, many of which have fallen into our hands; and from these one sees a tendency to gloat over the ghastly exhibits. The pictures portray gallows with a large number of natives hanging side by side. In some, soldiers are drawn up in hollow square, one side of it open to the civil population, and there is little doubt that these are punitive and impressive official executions, carried out under "proper judicial conditions" as conceived by Germans. But what offends one's taste so much are the photographs of German officers and men standing with self-conscious and self-satisfied expressions beside the grim gallows on which their victims hang. From the great number of these pictures we have found, it is quite clear that not only are such executions very common, but that they are also not unpleasing to the sense of the German population; otherwise they would not bequeath to posterity their own smiling faces alongside the unhappy dead. With us it is so different. When we have to administer the capital penalty we do it, of course, openly, and after full judicial inquiry in open court. Nor do we rob it of its impressive character by excluding the native population. But such sentences in war are usually carried out by shooting, and photographs are not desired by any of the spectators. It is a vile business and absolutely revolting to us, nor do we hesitate to hurry away as soon as the official character of the parade is over. I well remember one such execution, in Morogoro, of a German Askari who assaulted a little German girl with a "kiboko" during the two days' interregnum that elapsed between Lettow's departure and our occupation of the town. To British troops the most unwelcome duty of all is to form a part of a firing party on such occasions. The firing party are handed their rifles, alternate weapons only loaded with ball cartridge, that their sense of decency may not be offended by the distasteful recollection of killing a man in cold blood. For this assures that no man knows whether his was the rifle that sped the living soul from that pitiful cringing body.

In the past the Germans have had constant trouble with the natives, not one tribe but has had to be visited by sword and flame and wholesale execution. That this is not entirely the fault of the natives is shown by the fact that we have not experienced in East Africa and Uganda a tenth part of the trouble with our natives, notoriously a most restless and warlike combination of races.

It was thought at one time that, if the Germans seriously weakened their hold on some of the more troublesome tribes and withdrew garrisons from localities where troops alone had kept the native in subjection, risings of a terrible and embarrassing character would be the result. That such fear entered also into the German mind is shown by the fact that for long they did not dare to withdraw certain administrative officials, and much-valued soldiers of the regular army, who would have been of great service as army commanders, from their police work. Notably is this the case at Songea, in the angle between Lake Nyasa and the Portuguese border. To the state of terror among the German women owing to the fear of a native rising during the intervening period between the retreat of their troops and the arrival of our own in Morogoro I myself can testify. For the German nursing sisters who worked with me told of the flight to this town of outlying families, and how the women were all supplied with tablets of prussic acid to swallow, if the dreadful end approached. For death from the swift cyanide would be gentler far than at the hands of a savage native. But the Germans have to admit that as they showed no mercy to the native in the past, so they could expect none at such a time as this. They told me of the glad relief with which they welcomed the coming of our troops, and how with tears of gratitude they threw swift death into the bushes, much indeed as they hated the humiliating spectacle of the gallant Rhodesians and Baluchis making their formal entry into the fair streets of Morogoro.

The German hold on the natives is, owing to severe repressive measures in the past and the unrelaxing discipline of the present war, most effective and likely to remain so, until our troops appear actually among them. Indeed, the fear of a native rising, and the butchery of German women and children has been ever on our minds, and we have had to impress upon the native that we desired or could countenance no such help upon their part. All we asked of the native population was to keep the peace and supply us with information, food and porters. We sent word among the restless tribes to warn them to keep quiet, saying that, if the Germans had chastised them with whips, we would, indeed, chastise them with scorpions in the event of their getting out of hand. And we must admit that, almost without exception, the natives of all tribes have proved most welcoming, most docile and most grateful for our arrival. Had it not been for the clandestine intrigues of the German planters and missionaries whom we returned to their homes and occupations of peace, there would have been no trouble. But the Hun may promise faithfully, may enter into the most solemn obligations not to take active or passive part further in the war; but, nevertheless, he seems unable to keep himself from betraying our trust. Such a born spy and intriguer is he that he cannot refrain from intimidating the native, of whose quietness he is now assured by the presence of our troops, by threats of what will befall him when the Germans return, if he, the native, so much as sells us food or enters our employment as a porter.

But the native is extraordinarily local in his knowledge, his world bounded for him by the borders of neighbouring and often hostile tribes. We are not at all certain that any but coast or border tribes can really appreciate the difference between British rule and the domination that has now been swept away.

Recent reports on all sides show the desire for peace and the end of the war; for war brings in its train forced labour, the requisition of food, and the curse of German Askaris wandering about among the native villages, satisfying their every want, often at the point of the bayonet. Preferable even to this are the piping times of peace, when the German administrator, with rare exceptions, singularly unhappy in his dealing with the chiefs, would not hesitate to thrash a chief before his villagers, and condemn him to labour in neck chains, on the roads among his own subjects. And this, mark you, for the failure of the chief to keep an appointment, when the fat-brained German failed to appreciate the difference in the natives' estimation of time. By Swahili time the day commences at 7 a.m. In the past, it was no wonder that chiefs, burning with a sense of wrong and the humiliation they had suffered, preferred to raise their tribe and perish by the sword than endure a life that bore such indignity and shame.

But our job has not been rendered any easier by the difficulty we have experienced in pacifying the simple blacks by attempts to dispel the fears of rapine and murder at the hands of our soldiers, with which the Germans have been at such pains to saturate the native mind. This, in conjunction with the suspicion which the native of German East Africa has for any European, and more especially his horror of war, has made us prepared to see the native bolt at our approach.

But if our task has succeeded, there has been striking ill success on the part of the Germans in organising and inducing, in spite of their many attempts and the obvious danger to their own women and children, these native tribes to oppose our advance. Fortunately for us, and for the white women of the country, tribes will not easily combine, and are loath to leave their tribal territory.

Many of us have looked with some concern upon the mere possibility of this German colony being returned to its former owners. We must remember that we shall inevitably lose the measure of respect the native holds for us, if we contemplate giving back this province once more to German ruling. Prestige alone is the factor in the future that will keep order among these savage races who have now learnt to use the rifle and machine-gun, and have money in plenty to provide themselves with ammunition. The war has done much to destroy the prestige that allows a white man to dominate thousands of the natives. For to the indigenous inhabitants of the country, the white man's ways are inexplicable; they cannot conceive a war conducted with such alternate savagery and chivalry. To those who look upon the women of the vanquished as the victors' special prize, the immunity from outrage that German women enjoy is beyond their comprehension. For that reason we shall welcome the day when an official announcement is made that the British Government have taken over the country. One would like to see big "indabas" held at every town and centre in the country, formal raising of the Union Jack, cannon salutes, bands playing and parades of soldiers.

GOOD FOR EVIL

When the rains had finished, by May, 1916, in the Belgian Congo, General Molitor began to move upon Tanganyika. Soon our motor-boat flotilla and the Belgian launches and seaplanes had swept the lake of German shipping; and the first Belgian force landed and occupied Ujiji, the terminus of the Central Railway.

Then the blood of the Huns in Africa ran cold in their veins, and the fear that the advancing Belgians would wreak vengeance for the crimes of Germany in Belgium and to the Belgian consuls in prison in Tabora, gripped their vitals. Hastily they sent their women and children at all speed east along the line to Tabora, the new Provincial capital, and planned to put up the stiff rearguard actions that should delay the enemy, until the English might take Tabora and save their women from Belgian hands. For the English, those soft-hearted fools, who had already so well treated the women at Wilhelmstal, could be as easily persuaded to exercise their flabby sentimentalism on the women and children in Tabora. So ran the German reasoning.

Slowly and relentlessly the Belgian columns swept eastward along the railway line, closely co-operating with the British force advancing from Mwanza, southeast, toward the capital. But, in Molitor, the German General Wable had met more than his match, and soon, outgeneralled and out-manoeuvred, he had to rally on the last prepared position, west of Tabora. Then, daily, went the German parlementaires under the white flag, that standard the enemy know so well how to use, to the British General praying that he would occupy Tabora while Wable kept the Belgians in check. But the British General was adamant, and would have none of it; and as Wable's shattered forces fled to the bush to march south-east to where Lettow, the ever-vigilant, was keeping watch, the Belgians entered the fair city of Tabora. And here were over five hundred German women and children, clinging to the protection that the Governor's wife should gain for them. For Frau von Schnee was a New Zealand woman, and she might be looked to to persuade the British to restrain the Belgian Askari.

But there was no need. The behaviour of Belgian officers and their native soldiers was as correct and gentlemanly as that of officers should be, and, to their relief and surprise, those white women found the tables turned, and that their enemy could be as chivalrous to them as German soldiers--their own brothers--had been vile to the wretched people of Belgium. There was no nonsense about the Belgian General; stern and just, but very strict, he brought the German population to heel and kept them there. Cap in hand, the German men came to him, and begged to be allowed to work for the conqueror; their carpenters' shops, the blacksmiths' forges were at the service of the high commander. No German on the footpaths; hats raised from obsequious Teuton heads whenever a Belgian officer passes. How the chivalry of Belgium heaped coals of fire upon the German heads! And had the Hun been of such, a fibre as to appreciate the lesson, of what great value we might hope that it would be? But decent treatment never did appeal to the German; he always held that clemency spelt weakness, and the fear of the avenging German Michael. For did not the Emperor's Eagle now float over Paris and Petersburg? That he knew well; for had not High Headquarters told him of the message from the Kaiser by wireless from Nauen, the self-same message that conveyed to Lettow himself the Iron Cross decoration?

The Governor's wife was allowed to retain her palace and servants; but all German women were kept strictly to their houses after six at night. No looting, no riots, no disturbance. And German women began to be piqued at the calm indifference of smart Belgian officers to the favours they might have had. Openly chagrined were the local Hun beauties at such a disregard of their full-blown charms.

"I fear for our women and children in Tabora," said the German doctor to me in Morogoro. "Ach! what will the Belgians do when they hear the tales that are told of our German troops in Belgium? You don't believe these stories of German brutalities, do you?" he said anxiously, conciliatory. But I did, and I told him so. "But you don't know the Belgian Askari; he is cannibal; he is recruited from the pagan tribes in the forest of the Congo, he files his front teeth to a point, and we know he is short of supplies. What is going to happen to German children? It is the truth I tell you," he went on, evidently with very sincere feeling. "You know what became of the 1,500 Kavirondo porters your Government lent to the Belgian General. Where are our prisoners that the Belgians took in Ujiji and along the line? Eaten; all eaten." And he threw up his hands tragically to heaven. "I know you won't believe it, but

I swear to you that Rumpel's story is true." Rumpel was Lettow's best intelligence agent. "Our scout was a prisoner with a company of Belgian Askaris, you know, and it was only that the Belgian company commander wanted to get information from him that he was not eaten at once. Haven't you heard the tale that Rumpel tells after his escape? How the senior native officer came to his Belgian commander and complained that they had no food, the villages were empty, not so much as an egg or chicken to be got. Irritably, the Belgian officer shouted that the soldiers knew that no one had food, and they must wait till they got to the next post on the morrow. 'But,' urged the native sergeant softly, 'there are the prisoners.' 'Oh, the prisoners,' said the Belgian officer, relieved by an easy way out of a very difficult situation. 'Well, not more than sixteen, remember that.' And the sergeant went away."

This and countless other lies did the Germans tell us of our Belgian Allies. But how different the truth when it reached us at last along the railway by our troops that came from the northern column to join us at Morogoro. Not a German woman insulted; not one fat German child missing; no occupied house even entered by the Belgian troops, not so much as a chicken stolen from a German compound.

So just, so completely impartial was General Molitor, that he applied to German prisoners, in territory then occupied by him, the very rules and regulations that the German command had laid down for the governing of English and Belgian and other Allied prisoners. Only the vile, the unspeakable regulations, and every ordinance in that printed list of German rules that destroyed the prestige of the white man in the native's eyes, did he omit. If the Germans were indifferent to this one elementary rule of the white race in equatorial Africa--the white man's law that no white man be degraded before a native--then the Belgian would show the Hun how to play the game.

"We must hack our way through," said Bethmann-Hollweg. And we, in Morogoro, were very curious to see what manner of vengeance the Belgians might wreak. Nor would we have blamed them over-much for anything they might have done. I had lived in German prisons with elderly Belgian officers whose wives and grown-up daughters had been left behind in occupied parts of Belgium. We all had shuddered at the stories they told us; nor did we wonder that these unhappy fathers had often gone insane. And when we learnt the truth about Tabora, and knew too, to our disgust, that such un-German clemency was attributed to Belgian fear of the avenging German Michael and not to natural Belgian chivalry, we were furious. What can one do with such a people?

THE MECHANICAL TRANSPORT

A cloud of red dust along a rough bush track, a rattling jar approaching, and the donkey transport pulls into the bushes to let the Juggernaut of the road go by. Swaying and plunging over the rough ground, lurches one of our huge motor lorries. Perched high up upon the seat, face and arms burnt dark brown by the tropical sun, is the driver. Stern faced and intent upon the road, he slews his big ship into a better bit of road by hauling at the steering wheel. Beside him on the seat the second driver. Ready to their hands the rifles that may save their precious cargo from the marauding German patrol which lies hidden in the thick bush beside the road. In the big body of the car behind are two thousand pounds of rations, and atop of all a smiling "tota," the small native boy these drivers employ to light their fires and cook their food at night. And this load is food for a whole brigade alone for half a day; so you may see how necessary it is that this valuable cargo arrives in time.

It may sound to you, in sheltered London, a pleasant and agreeable thing to drive through this strange new country full of the wild game that glimpses of Zoological Gardens in the past suggest. "A Zoo without a blooming keeper." But there is no department of war that does such hard work as these lorry drivers.

For them no rest in the day that is deemed a lucky one, if it provides them only with sixteen hours' work. The infantry of the line have their periodical rests, a month it may be, of comparative leisure before the enemy trenches. But for mechanical transport there is no peace, save such as comes when back axles break, and the big land ship is dragged into the bush to be repaired. Hot and sweating men striving to renew some part or improvise, by bullock hide "reims," a temporary road repair that will bring them limping back to the advance base. Here the company workshop waits to repair these derelicts of the road. Burning with malaria, when the hot sun draws the lurking fever from their bones, tortured with dysentery, they've got to do their job until they reach their lorry park again. But often the repair gang cannot reach a stranded lorry, and the drivers, helpless before a big mechanical repair, have to camp out alongside their car, till help arrives and tows them in. A tarpaulin rigged up along one side of the lorry, poles cut from the thorn bush, and they have protection from the burning sun by day. A thorn hedge, the native "boma," keeps out lions and the sneaking hyaena at night. Nor are their rifles more than a half protection, for the '303 makes so clean a hole that it is often madness to attempt to shoot a lion with it. Once wounded he is far more dangerous a foe. Here the "tota" earns his pay, for he can hunt the native villages for "cuckoos," the native fowls, and eggs.

The load of rations must not, save at the last extremity, be broached.

And the roads they travel on: you never saw such things, mere bush tracks where the pioneers have cut down trees and bushes, and left the stumps above the level earth. No easy job to steer these great lumbering machines between these treacherous stumps. From early dawn to late night you'll meet these leviathans of the road, diving into the bush to force a new road for themselves when the old track is too deep in mud or dust, plunging and diving down water-courses or the rocky river-beds, creeping with great care over the frail bridge that spans a deep ravine. A bridge made up of tree-trunks laid lengthwise on wooden up-rights. The lion and the leopard stand beside the road, with paw uplifted, in the glare of the headlights at night.

Nor is there only danger from flood and fever and the denizens of the forest. There is ever to be feared the lurking German patrol that trains its dozen rifles upon the driver, knowing full well that he must sit and quietly face it out, or the lorry, once out of control, plunges against a tree and becomes, with both its drivers, the prey of these marauders. So, while his mate fumbles with the bolt lever of his rifle, the driver takes a firmer grip of the wheel, gives her more "juice," and plunges headlong down the road. At Handeni I once had a driver with five bullets in him; they had not stopped him until he reached safety, and his mate was able to take over. Nor does this exhaust the risks of his job, for there is the land mine, buried in the soft dust of the road, or beneath the crazy bridge. Laid at night by the patrol that harasses our lines of communication, they are the special danger of the first convoy to come along the road in the morning. Troops we have not to spare to guard these long lines of ours, so, in particularly dangerous places, the driver carries a small guard of soldiers on the top of his freight behind him. Native patrols, very wise at noticing any derangement of the surface dust, patrol the highways at dawn to lift these unwelcome souvenirs from the roads.

From South Africa, from home, and from Canada, come the drivers and mechanics of the motor transport. The Canadians, stout fellows from Toronto, Winnipeg, and the Far West, enlisted in the British A.S.C. in Canada, and arrived in England only to be sent to East Africa. It seems at first sight a strange country to which to send these men from the north, but in fact it was a very happy choice. For they got away from the cold dampness of England and Flanders into the summer seas of the South Atlantic, where the flying fish and rainbow nautilus filled them with surprise. Cape Town and Durban must have been for these Canadian lads a new world only previously envisaged by them, in the big all-red map that hangs on the walls of Canadian schools, A little difficult at first, apt to chafe at the restrictions that, though perhaps not necessary for themselves in particular, were yet essential in preserving discipline in the whole mixed unit, rather inclined to resent certain phases of soldier life. But soon they settled down to do their job, to take trouble over their work rather than make trouble by grousing over it. Well they proved their worth by the number that now fill the non-commissioned ranks, and may be judged by the commendation of their commanding officers. I used to think that they came to see me in particular, at the long sick parades I held in Morogoro and Handeni, because I too lived, like some of them, in British Columbia. I cannot flatter my soul by thinking that they came for the special quality of the quinine or medical advice I dished out to them. It may have been that they were far from home, and I seemed a friend in a very strange land.

All I know is, that I felt a great compliment was paid to me that they should be grateful for the often hurried and small attentions that I could give them. They would sometimes bring me Canadian papers that took me back two and a half years, to the time when I came to England on a six weeks' holiday from my work, a holiday that has now spun out to three and a half years, and shows every sign of going further still. Very well these men stood the climate, in spite of their fair colouring, in a country that penalises the blonde races more than the brown, that makes us pay for our want of protective pigment. One stout fellow I well remember, who had acute appendicitis at Morogoro, was the driver, or engineer as they are called, of a Grand Trunk Pacific train that ran from Edmonton in Alberta to Prince Rupert on the Pacific. We operated upon him, and, though he did very well, yet he must have suffered many things from our want of nursing in his convalescence. Very considerate and uncomplaining he was, like all the good fellows in our hospital, giving no trouble, and making every allowance for our difficulties. In fact, the great trouble one has among soldiers, is to get them to make any complaint to their own medical officer. If one suggests things to them or asks them leading questions, they will sometimes admit to certain deficiencies in food or treatment by the orderlies. But of what one did oneself or what the German sister left undone, there was never a complaint to me; though I rather think there were many grouses when once they left the hospital. It seemed to me that it was not that they didn't know better, or that they didn't know that certain things were wrong, for it is a very intelligent army, this of ours, and has been in hospital before in civil life, but all along I felt that they did not like to hurt one's feelings by not getting well as quickly as they might, and that they often pretended to a degree of comfort and ease from pain that I'm sure was not the fact. But this phase is often met with in civil life too, a doctor has much to be grateful for that many of his patients insist on getting well or saying that they are better, just to please him.

The German surgical sister was always kind to our men, and when the serious state of the wound was past she would do the dressings herself, while I went about some other work. Our men liked her, and I remember that our Canadian engine driver offered her, in his kindly way, to give her a free pass on the Grand Trunk Railway. He little knew that this German sister represented no small part of two big German shipping companies that could once have provided her with free passes over any railway in the world. I had under me, too, a couple of Canadian drivers whose lorry in crossing one of the ramshackle bridges over a river, hit the railing on the side and plunged to the rocky depths below. A loose tree-trunk that formed the roadbed of the bridge had jerked the steering wheel from the driver's hands. Over went the lorry on top of them, and the mercy of Providence only interposed a big rock that left room below for the two drivers to escape the crushing that would have killed them. Badly bruised only, they left me later to recover of their contusion in the hospital at Dar-es-Salaam.

THE SURGERY OF THIS WAR

"Please give us a drop of Johnnie Walker before you do my dressing," said my Irish sergeant, who had lost his leg in the fight at Kangata. Lest you might think that by "Johnnie Walker" he asked for his favourite brand of whiskey, I may tell you that we had no stimulant of that kind with us. It was chloroform he wanted to dull the pain that dressing his severed nerves entailed. Always full of cheer and blarney, he kept our ward alive, only when the time for daily dressing came round did his countenance fall. Then anxious eyes begged for ease from pain. But this once over, he laid his tired dirty face upon the embroidered pillow and jested of all the things the careful German housewife would say could she but see her embroidered sheets and the blue silk cushion from her drawing-room that kept his amputated leg from jars. We had no water to wash the men, barely enough for cooking and for surgical dressings, but there were silk bedspreads and eiderdown quilts and all the treasures of German sitting-rooms. And the fact that they were taken from the Germans was balm to these wounded men.

There was Murray, a regimental sergeant-major, his leg badly broken by the lead slug from a German Askari's rifle, ever the fore-most at the padre's services, chanting the responses and leading all the hymns. And Wehmeyer, the young Boer, who had accidentally blown a great hole through his leg above the ankle joint. And Green, the Rhodesian sergeant who had been brought in, almost *in extremis*, with blackwater. Nor was his condition improved by the experience of having been blown up in the ambulance by a land mine, hidden in the thick dust of the road. Thrown into the air by the force of the explosion, the car had turned over on him and the driver, who was killed. And there was Becker the blue-eyed German prisoner with a bullet through his femoral artery and his hip. Blanched from loss of blood before I could tie the vessel and stanch the bleeding, his leg suspended in our improvised splints, and on his way to make a splendid recovery. And Taube, another German prisoner, shot through the abdomen, and recovering after his operation. Gentle and conciliatory, with eyes of a frightened rabbit, he was the son of the great Taube, the physiologist of Dresden.

Cheek by jowl, in the best bed, was Zahn, the hated Ober-Leutenant, loathed by his own men, one of whom wrote in his diary that he loved to see the bombardment of Tanga, "for Zahn was there, the ----, and I hope he'll meet a 12-inch shell." Jealous of his officer's prerogative, and disinclined to be nursed in the same ward with our soldiers and his own, he gave a lot of trouble, demanding inordinately, victimising our orderly, unashamedly selfish. But he was sheltered from my wrath by the grave gunshot wound of his thigh. Cowardly under suffering, he was in striking contrast to Becker, who stood graver pain with hardly a flinch. After a great struggle he was eventually moved to Korogwe to the stationary hospital. There it became necessary to amputate his leg, and Zahn surrendered what little courage he had left. "No leg to-night, no Zahn to-morrow," he said to his nurse. And he was right, for at eleven that night he had no leg, and at two the next morning there was no Zahn upon this earth.

And there was Sergeant Eve of the South African Infantry, who got a D.C.M., a Londoner, and of unquenchable good humour. Vastly pleased with the daily bottle of stout we got for him with such difficulty, from supplies, he faced the awful daily dressing of his shattered leg without flinching, pretending to great comfort and an excellent position of his splint, which his crooked leg and my practised eye belied.

And there was Smith, yet a boy, but who always felt "champion" and "quite comfortable," though his days were few in the land and his pain must have been very severe. Yet in his case he had days of that merciful euthanasia, the wonderful ease from pain that sometimes lasts for days before the end. In great contrast with these was an individual with a wound through the fleshy part of the thigh, by far the least seriously wounded of all in the ward, who never failed with his unending requests to the patient orderlies and his eternal complainings, until a public dressing-down from me brought him to heel. And Glover who wept that I had lost his bullet, that unforgivable carelessness in a surgeon that allows a bullet, removed at an operation, to be thrown away with discarded dressings.

But, of all, the perfect prince was De La Motte, a subaltern in the 29th Punjabis, ever the leader of the dangerous patrols along the native bush paths that give themselves so readily to ambush. Shot through the spine and paralysed below the waist his life was only a question of months. But if he had little time to live, he had determined to see it through with a gay courage that was wonderful to see. Previously wounded in France, he yet seemed, though he cannot possibly have been in ignorance, to be buoyed up with the perfect faith in recovery with which fractured spines so often are endowed; never asking me awkward questions, he made it so easy for me to do his daily dressing, so grateful for small attentions, and so ready to believe me when I told him that it was only a question of weeks before he would be home again. And in spite of all fears I have just heard he did get home to see his people, and by his cheerful courage to rob Death of all his terrors.

MY OPERATING THEATRE AT HANDENI

Up the wide stone steps, under the arch of purple Bougainvillea and you are in my operating theatre. A curtain of mosquito gauze screens it from the vulgar gaze. Behind these big wooden doors a week ago was the office of this erstwhile German jail. To the left and right, now all clean and white painted, were the living rooms of the German jailor and his wife, but for the present they are transformed into special wards for severely wounded men. On the lime-washed wall and very carefully preserved is " ***Gott strafe England***" which the late occupants wrote in charcoal as they fled. Strange how all German curses come home to roost, and move us to the ridicule that hurts the Hun so much and so surely penetrates his pachydermatous hide. That the "Hymn of Hate" should be with us a cause for jest, and "strafe" be adopted, with enthusiasm, into the English language, he cannot understand. To him, as often to our own selves, we shall always be incomprehensible.

Through the gauze screen on to the white operating table passed all the flotsam of wounded humanity in the summer months. All the human wreckage that marked the savage bush fighting from German Bridge to Morogoro came to me upon this table. And its white cleanness, our towels and surgical gloves and overalls, filled them with a sense of comfort and of safety after weary and perilous journeys, that was in no way detracted from by the gleaming instruments laid out beside the table. Even this chamber of pain was a haven of refuge to these broken men after long jolting rides over execrable roads.

But a particularist among surgeons would have found much to disapprove of in this room. Cracks in the stone floor let in migrating bands of red ants that no disinfectant would drive away. Arrow slit windows, high up in the walls, gave ingress to the African swallow, redheaded and red-backed, whose tuneful song was a perpetual delight. His nests adorned the frieze, but they were full of squeaking youngsters and we could not shut the parents out. So we banished them during operating hours by screens of mosquito gauze; and to reward us, they sang to our bedridden men from ward window-sills.

But despite these shortcomings of the operating theatre itself, we did good work here, and got splendid results. For God was good, and the clean soil took pity upon our many deficiencies. Earth, that in France or Gallipoli hid the germs of gangrene and tetanus, here merely produced a mild infection. Lucky for us that we did not need to inject the wounded with tetanus antitoxin. But an added charm was given to our work by the necessity of improvisation. Broken legs were put up in plaster casings with metal interruptions, so that the painful limb might be at rest, and yet the wound be free for daily dressings. The Huns left us plaster of Paris, damp indeed but still serviceable after drying; the corrugated iron roofing of the native jail provided us with the necessary metal. Then by metal hoops the leg was slung from home-made cradles, and I defy the most modern hospital to show me anything more comfortable or efficient. Broken thighs were suspended in slings from poles above the bed, painted the red, white and black that marked German Government Survey posts. Naturally in a field hospital such as this, we had no nurses; but our orderlies, torn from mine shafts of Dumfriesshire and the engine sheds of the North British Railway, did their best, and compensated by much kindliness for their lack of nursing training.

Sadly in need were we of trained nurses; for the bedsores that developed in the night were a perpetual terror. Ring pillows we made out of grass and bandages, but a fractured thigh, as you know, must lie upon his back, and we had little enough rectified spirit to harden the complaining flesh. But nurses we could not have at so advanced a post as this. The saving factor of all our work lay in the natural goodness of the men. They felt that many things were not right; for ours is a highly intelligent army and knows more of medicine and surgery than we, in our blindness, realise. But they made light of their troubles, as they learnt the difficulties we laboured with. So grateful were they for small attentions. That we should go out of our way to take pains to obtain embroidered sheets and lace-edged pillows, absolved us in their eyes from all the want of surgical nursing. Liberal morphia we had to give to compensate for nursing defects. I have long felt that I would rather work for sick soldiers than for any class of humanity; and in fifteen years I have come to know the sick human animal in all his forms. So that the least that one could do was to scheme to get the precious egg by private barter with the natives, and to find the silk pillow that spelt comfort, but was the anathema of asepsis. No wonder that such splendid and uncomplaining victims spurred us to our best endeavours and made of toil a very joy.

SOME AFRICAN DISEASES

This is the season of blackwater fever, the pestilence that stalks in the noontide and the terror of tropical campaigning. Hitherto with the exception of the Rhodesians who have had this disease previously in their northern territory, or men who have come from the Congo or the shores of the Great Lakes, our army has been fairly free from this dread visitation. The campaigning area of the coast and the railway line of British East Africa that gave our men malaria in plenty during the first two years of war, had not provided many of those focal areas in which this disease is distributed. The Loyal North Lancashires and the 25th Royal Fusiliers had been but little affected. The Usambara Valley along the Tanga-Moschi railway was also fairly free. On the big trek from Kilimanjaro to Morogoro the blackwater cases were almost entirely confined to Rhodesians and to the Kashmiris, who suffer in this way in their native mountains of Nepal. But once we struck the Central Railway and penetrated south towards the delta of the Rufigi the tale was different. British and South African troops began to arrive in the grip of this fell malady. It was written on their faces as they were lifted from ambulance or mule waggon. There was no need to seek the cause in the scrap of paper that was the sick report. All who ran could read it in the blanched lips, the grey-green pallor of their faces, the jaundiced eye, the hurried breathing. Thereupon came three days' struggle with Azrael's pale shape before the blackwater gave place to the natural colour again, or until the secreting mechanism gave up the contest altogether and the Destroying Angel settled firmly on his prey. At first, if there was no vomiting, it was easy to ply the hourly drinks of tea and water and medicine. But once deadly and exhausting vomiting had begun, one could no longer feed the victim by the mouth. Then came the keener struggle for life, for fluid was essential and had to be given by other ways and means. Into the soft folds of the skin of the arm-pits, breast and flanks we ran in salt solution by the pint. The veins of the arms we brought into service, that we might pour in this vitalising fluid. Day and night the fight goes on for three days, until it is won or lost. Here again, as in tick fever, we use the preparation 606, for which we are indebted to the great Ehrlich. Champagne is a great stand-by. So well recognised is the latter remedy that all old hands at tropical travel take with them a case of "bubbly water" for such occasions as these. Blessed morphia, too, brings ease of vomiting and is a priceless boon.

You ask me the cause of this disease, and I have to admit that among the authorities themselves there are no settled convictions. Some hold--and for my part I am with them--that the attack is caused by quinine given in too large a dose to a subject who is rotten with malaria. But there are others who maintain that it is a malarial manifestation only, and that the big dose of quinine, which seems to some to precipitate the attack, is only a coincidence. Be that as it may, there is little difference in the treatment adopted by either school. Death achieves his victory as frequently with one as with another. Certain it is that, to the common mind, quinine is the reputed cause and is avoided in large doses by men who have once had blackwater, or who are in that low rotten state that predisposes to it. In one point all agree, that one must be saturated with malaria before blackwater can develop. So great is the aversion shown by some men to the big doses of quinine as laid down by regulations, that men have often refused to take their quinine. Others, too, who have protested at first, take their quinine ration only to find themselves in the grip of this disease within twelve hours. Such a case was a Frenchman named Canarie (and the colour of his face, upon admission, did not belie his name), who had been treated for blackwater fever by the great Koch in Uganda many years before, and had been warned by him against big doses of quinine. That evening he was on my hands, fortunately soon to recover, and to win a prolonged convalescent leave out of this rain to the sunny and non-malarial slopes of Wynberg.

Seldom do the rumbling ambulances roll in but among their human freight is some poor wretch snoring into unconsciousness or in the throes of epileptiform convulsions. Custom has sharpened our clinical instinct, and where, in civil life, we would look for meningitis, now we only write cerebral malaria, and search the senseless soldier's pay-book for the name that we may put upon the "dangerous list." As this name is flashed 12,000 miles to England, I sometimes wonder what conception of malaria his anxious relatives can have.

For there is no aspect of brain diseases that cerebral malaria cannot simulate; deep coma or frantic struggling delirium. A drop of blood from the lobe of the ear and the microscope reveals the deadly "crescents"--the form the subtertian parasite assumes in this condition. No time this for waiting or expectant treatment. Quinine must be given in huge doses, regardless of the danger of blackwater, and into the muscles or, dissolved in salt solution, into the veins. The Germans have left me some fine hollow needles that practice makes easy to pass into the distended swollen veins. Through this needle large doses of quinine are injected, and in six hours usually no crescent remains to be seen. As a rule, conscious life returns to these senseless bodies after some hours; but, unhappily, such success does not always crown our efforts. Then it is the padre's turn, and in the cool of the following afternoon the firing party, with arms reversed, toils behind our sky-pilot to that graveyard on the sunlit slopes of Mount Uluguru, where our surgical failures are put to rest.

One can always tell, you know, the onset of such a complication as this; for when one finds the victim of malaria hazy and stupid after his fever has abated; and, more especially, if he develops wandering tendencies, leaving his stretcher at night to choose another bed in the ward, often to the protesting consternation of its present occupant, then one passes the word to Sister Elizabeth to get the transfusion apparatus ready. I shall not readily forget one stout fellow, a white company sergeant-major in the Gold Coast Regiment, who was lost in the bush and discovered after many days in the grip of this fell disease. Him they bore swiftly to me at Handeni, and after many injections and convulsions innumerable, he was restored to conscious life again. Sent back by me eventually to Korogwe with a letter advising his invaliding out of the country, he opened and read my report upon the way. But he was of those who do not take kindly to invaliding. Who would run his machine-gun section, if he were away, and his battalion in action? Who like he could know the language and the little failings of his dusky machine-gun crew that he had trained so long and so carefully in the Cameroon? So he appeared in the books of the Stationary Hospital at Korogwe as an ordinary case of convalescent malaria on his own statement. And when they would send him still further back to M'buyuni he broke out from hospital one night, and, with his native orderly, boarded the train to Railhead and marched the other 200 miles to Morogoro. Here I met him on the road starting out on the next long trek of 125 miles to Kissaki. For news had come to him that the Gold Coast Regiment had been in action and their impetuous courage rewarded by captured enemy guns and a long casualty list. But he was determined and unrepentant, one of his beloved machine-guns had been put out of action. How could I hold him back? So joining forces with another white sergeant of his regiment, who was hardly recovered from a wound, these two good fellows set out with a note that, *this* time, was not to be destroyed, for the instruction of their regimental doctor.

A third scourge responsible for frequent admissions into hospital is "tick-fever." Rather an unpleasant name, isn't it? And in its course and effect it fully acts up to its reputation. More commonly known as "relapsing fever," this illness attacks men who have been sleeping on the floor of native huts, which in this country are swarming with these parasites. Once in seven days for five or seven weeks these men burn with high fever--higher and more violent even than malaria--but sooner over. As you may imagine, it leaves them very debilitated; for no sooner does the victim recover from one attack than another is due. The ticks that are the host of the spirillum, the actual cause of the disease, live in the soft earth on the floor of native huts at the junction of the vertical cane rods and the soil. Here, by scraping, you may discover hundreds of these loathsome beasts in every foot of wall. But they are fortunately different from the grass ticks that, though unpleasant, are not dangerous to man. For the tick that carries the spirillum is blind and cannot climb any smooth surface. So to one sleeping on a bed or even a native "machela" above the ground, he is harmless. But woe betide the tired soldier who attempts to escape the tropical rain by taking refuge on the floor. In sleep he is attacked, and when his blind assailant is full of blood he drops off; so the soldier may never know that he has been bitten. I got twelve cases alone from one company of the Rhodesians, who sheltered in a native village near Kissaki. Of course, not every tick is infected, and for that we have to be very grateful. At the height of the fever the spirillum appears in the blood as an attenuated, worm-like creature, actively struggling and squirming among the blood corpuscles. A drop of blood taken from the ear shows hundreds of these young snakes beneath the microscope. For the cure we are again indebted to that excellent Hun bacteriologist Ehrlich, who gave us .606--a strong arsenical preparation that we dissolve in a pint of salt solution, and inject into the veins at the height of the paroxysm of fever. This definitely destroys the spirillum, and no further attacks of fever result; but this injection, once its work is done, does not confer immunity from other attacks. It is typical of the Hun and his anti-Semitic feelings that Ehrlich, the most distinguished of German scientists, perhaps, after Koch, has never received the due reward of all the distinction he has conferred on German medicine, for the offence that he was a Jew. We should have honoured him, as we have done Jenner or Lister.

Relapsing, or **Rueckfall** fever, as the Germans call it, was one of the common dodges used by them to deceive the ingenuous British doctor. For the subtle Hun prisoner knew that, if he pretended to this disease, it would win him at least a week in the grateful comfort of a hospital, and perchance the ministering joys conferred by German nursing sisters, until the expected relapse did not occur; then the British doctor, realising the extent of his deception, would thrust these shameless malingerers to the cold comfort of the prison camp.

How is it, you might ask me, that there are any natives left, if tropical Africa is so full of such beastly diseases as this? Is it that the native is naturally immune, or is it that the white man is of such a precious quality that he alone is attacked by these parasites and poisonous biting flies? The fact is that the native is affected also, and in childhood chiefly, so that the infant mortality in many native tribes is very high. And there is little doubt that repeated attacks of malaria in youth, if recovered from, do confer a kind of protection against attacks in adult life. But this is not the case with newly introduced disease; for the sleeping sickness that came to Uganda along the caravan routes from the Congo, has swept away fully a million of the natives along the shores of Lake Victoria Nyanza.

But the native has a sure sense of the unhealthiness of any locality, and one must be prepared for trouble when one notices that the native villages are built up on the hillsides. This was specially remarked by us on our long trek down the Pangani, and thus we were warned of the fever that lurked in the bright green lush meadows beside the water, and the "fly" that soon overtook our transport mules and cattle and the horses of General Brits' 2nd Mounted Brigade. At first we thought the columns of smoke along the mountain-sides beside the Pangani were signal fires for the enemy; but before long, when the roads were choked with victims of "fly" and horse-sickness, we realised the wisdom that induced the simple native to take his sheep and cattle up the hillsides and above the danger zone. When one spends only a short time in some native huts, it is quite clear how he escapes infection. For the floor is covered with a layer of wood ashes that is usually deadly to bugs and fleas and ticks and other crawling beasts; and the atmosphere is so full of wood smoke that the most enterprising mosquito or tsetse-fly would flee, as we do, choking from the acrid smoke. So the native fire that burns within his hut day and night not only serves to cook his food and to keep wild beasts away, but also supplies him with an excellent form of Keating's Powder for the floor and smoke to drive the winged insects from the grateful warmth of his fireside.

HORSE-SICKNESS

Lying beside the road with outstretched neck and a spume of white froth on nose and muzzle are the horses of the 2nd Mounted Brigade; with bodies swollen by the decomposition that sets in so rapidly in this sun, and smelling to high heaven, are the fine young horses that came so gallantly through Kahe some ten days ago. "Brits' violets" the Tommies call them, as they seek a site to windward to pitch their tents. "Hyacinths" they mutter, as the wind changes in the night, and drives them choking from their blankets, illustrating the truth of the South African "Kopje-Book" maxim, "One horse suffices to move a camp--if he be dead enough." For weeks after the Brigade passed through M'Kalamo the air was full of stench, and the bush at night alive with lions coming for the feast. For this is horse-sickness, the plague that strikes an apparently healthy horse dead in his tracks, while the Boer trooper hastily removes bridle and saddle and picks another horse from the drove of remounts that follow after. No time to drag the body off the road; so the huge motor lorries choose another track in the bush to avoid this unwholesome obstruction.

Horse-sickness takes ten short days to develop after infection, and the organism is so tiny that it passes through the finest filter and is ultramicroscopic. That means that it is too small to be recognised by the high power of an ordinary micro-scope. There was horse-sickness in the bush meadows beside the river near Kahe. Careless troopers watered their horses, after sundown, when the dew was on the grass and death lurked in the evening moisture where it had been absent in the dry heat of the afternoon.

THE WOUNDED FROM KISSAKI

Two very busy days were before us when the wounded came in from Kissaki, so badly shaken and so pale and wan after their journey. They had been cared for by the Field Ambulance before I got them, and by the extraordinary excellence of the surgery paid the greatest of tributes to the care of the surgeons in front. The Ger-man hospital there, half finished--for our advance had been far ahead of German calculations-- fell into our hands and with it a German doctor and some nurses. The nurses had been very kind to our men and worked well for our doctors, but they had followed the usual German custom in this country, of being too liberal with morphia. That this drug can become a curse is well known, though it is, when given in reason, the greatest blessing, the most priceless boon of war. One feels perhaps that the sisters had given it without the surgeon's knowledge, and not entirely to give ease from pain, but also perhaps to give rest to the ward, the quiet that would allow these over-worked women to get some sleep themselves. It was written on the faces of the three amputation cases that they had had too much morphia. And as this drug robs men of their appetite, keeps them thin, and prevents their wounds from healing, it became my unpleasant task to break them of it. This was only to be done by hardening one's heart, by giving bromide and stout, and insisting on the egg and milk that interspaced all meals. It is so easy to get a reputation for kindness by being too complacent in giving way to requests for morphia. It made one feel such an absolute brute to disregard the wistful pleading eye, the hands that tugged at the mosquito curtains to show they were awake, when, late at night, I made my evening round. But it had to be done, and I fear the work and the sun and the trop-ics made one's temper very short, particularly when it was only possible by losing one's temper to preserve the indifference to these influences that was necessary to complete the cure. It was very hard on them at the time, especially as they were rotten with malaria and tick fever, in addition to their wounds. But there were other ways in which one made it up to them, if they did but know it. Nor did they see that quinine given by the veins, so much more trouble to me and to the sister, was better for them than the quinine tablet that was so easily swallowed, and so ineffectual. Nor could they, one thought, always know that 606 had to be given for tick fever, and that it was of no value save when given at the height of fever, when they felt so miserable and so disinclined to be disturbed.

There was Shelley, the Irishman, a big policeman from Johannesburg, badly wounded in the thigh. He had been taken prisoner by the Germans and remained so for three days, until our next advance found him installed in the German hospital. His wound was so bad that amputation alone was left to do. When the worst of the dressings was over and the stage of daily change of gauze and bandage had arrived, he always liked Sister Elizabeth to do his dressings. Sister's hands were much more gentle than mine, and Shelley always associated me with pain, little knowing that, if a dressing is to be well and properly done, it is always inseparable from a certain amount of suffering. But I saw through his blarney, and he was added to the list of those who preferred sister's hands to my attentions.

And there was Rose, a mere lad, who had also lost a leg from wounds; he lay awake at night, though not in great pain, during the process of breaking him of the morphia habit. When I pretended not to hear his little moan, as I made my evening round, he tugged at his mosquito curtain to show that he was awake. But asperin and bromide and a nightly drink of hot brandy and water soon broke off this habit. After that it was easy to cut off the alcohol by degrees as he grew to like his eggs in milk the more. He, too, always had some reason why Sister should do his dressings, and I think that Sister Elizabeth and he plotted together that I should have some other more important job to do when Rose's turn came to go upon the table.

Then there was Parsons, the printer, who in times of peace produced the **_Rand Daily Mail_**; he had also lost a leg and he surprised me with his special knowledge of the various qualities of paper.

In the corner of the verandah that had been turned into an extra ward by screening it off with native reed-fencing was Gilfillan, the most perfect patient. Propping his foot against the wall to correct the foot-drop that division of the nerve of his leg had caused, he had passed many sleepless nights in his long and wearisome convalescence.

Beside the door, beckoning to me in a mysterious manner, was Drury, a trooper in the South African Horse. In his eyes a suspicious light, as he earnestly requested to be moved. "For God's sake take me away, they're trying to poison my food; and those Germans over there are going to shoot me to-night." This poor lad had been shot badly through the shoulder, and only by the skill of Moffat, the surgeon from Cape Town, had he retained what was left of his shattered arm. Now malaria, in addition, had him in its grip, and his mental condition told me plainly that his brain was being affected. With the greatest difficulty Sister Elizabeth and I persuaded him to undergo the quinine transfusion into his veins that restored him to sober sense the next day. "I really did think those two German prisoners were going to shoot me," he said. But the two prisoners in his ward were more afraid of him than he of them, and their broken legs, for they had got in the way of one of our machine-guns, precluded any movement from their beds. Our men were extraordinarily kind to German prisoners in the ward. The Boers were different; they were never unkind, but they ignored them completely, for the Union of South Africa had too much to forgive in the Rebellion and in German South-West Africa. "Now then, Fritz, there ain't no bleeding sausage for you this morning;" and Fritz, smilingly obedient, stretched out his hand for the cold bacon that was his breakfast. Toward the end Sister Hildegarde was just as kind to our men as she was to her own people, and she was highly indignant with me when I stopped the night orderly from waking her, early one morning, when I had to transfuse a blackwater case with salt solution. She thought, she who had had quite enough to do the day before, that I did not call her because I thought she did not want to get up. She felt that I was tacitly drawing a distinction between her conduct of that morning and the self-denial of the other night, when she and Elizabeth sat up all night and day with a German soldier who had perforated his intestines during an attack of typhoid fever. I had operated upon him to close the hole the typhoid ulcer had made. The German doctor, to whom we had given his liberty, in order that he might attend the civil population, and whom I had called in consultation over the case, had disagreed with our diagnosis. But I had overruled him, and at the operation was glad to be able to show him and the German sisters that our diagnosis was right, and that I was not operating on him just because he happened to be a prisoner of war. The German sisters were grateful to us for getting up at night and in the early morning to give him the salt solution that might save his life, and they repaid it in the only way they could, by kindness to our men. But in any case they could not help liking our sick soldiers, and many is the time that they have been indignant with me for deficiencies in food and equipment which I could not help. "Our German soldiers would have complained until their cries reached Lettow himself," they said, "if they had to put up with what you make your soldiers endure."

And if, at first, Hildegarde, of the sour and disapproving face, did little irregular things for wounded German soldiers, faked temperature charts, prepared little forbidden meals at night, and in other ways pretended to a degree of illness in her German soldiers that my clinical eye refused to see, I could not altogether blame her. When I remembered the treatment that I saw our sick and wounded prisoners in Germany get from the Hun doctor, I was often furious, and determined to do a bit of "strafing" on my own. But I could not forget that the French and Belgian nurses did just the same for our wounded in German hands, adding bandages to unwounded limbs, describing to the German doctor our sleepless nights of pain when the walls of that French convent had echoed only to our snores, preparing delicious feasts, at night, for us to compensate for German rations, and in many ways contriving to keep us longer in their hands and to postpone the journey that would land us in the vileness of a German prison hospital. Hildegarde had her troubles too, for she had not heard for two years of her lover in Germany, whose mild and bespectacled face peered from a photograph in her room. He did not look to be made of heroic mould, but who can tell? Long ago he may have bitten the dust of Flanders or found another sweetheart to console him. And the native hospital boys, swift to recognise the changes of war and the comparative leniency of British discipline, got out of hand and failed to clean and scrub as they did in former days. Then I would inquire and uphold Hildegarde, and the recalcitrant Mahomed would be marched off to receive fifteen of the best from the Provost Sergeant.

MY OPERATING THEATRE IN MOROGORO

"Jambo bwona," and the sycophantic Ali would leap to his feet and raise the dirty red fez that adorned his head. "Jambo," said Nazoro, the senior boy, standing to attention. For Nazoro was a Wanyamwezi from Lake Tanganyika and disdained any of Ali's dodges to conciliate me. Graceful as a deer was Nazoro, and a good Askari lost in a better operating-room boy. This was my morning greeting as I peeped in before breakfast to see that the operating theatre was swept and garnished for the day's work. "Good morning," said Elizabeth, looking up from the steriliser where she was preparing instruments for the morning operations.

Educated partly in England and speaking the language perfectly, she hated us only a little less than the other Germans. But she was good at her job and conscientious, and a very great help to us. Always as cheerful as one could expect a woman to be who worked for the English soldiers and dressed the wounds of men to fit them to return to the field to fight against her people again. Who knows that the tall Rhodesian, from whose feet she so skilfully removed the "jiggers" and cleansed the wounds of a long trek, would not, all the sooner for her care, perhaps be drawing a bead upon her husband in the near future? Very proud was Elizabeth of her husband's Iron Cross that the Kaiser had sent by wireless only last week; news of which was told to her by a wounded prisoner just brought in. For her husband, who, to judge from his wife's description, must have been quite a good fellow for a Hun, was in command of one of the "Schutzen" companies down near the Rufigi. He, too, had lived long in England to learn the ways of English shipping companies that would prove of such value to the Deutsch Ost-Afrika Line. So jubilant was she at the news that I had to give her a half-holiday to recover; twice only in the four months we worked together was Elizabeth as happy: once when she got a letter, by the infinite kindness of General Smuts, from her husband, and another time when a letter came from Switzerland to tell her of her baby in Hamburg, her mother, and the two brothers that were in the cavalry in the advance into Russia. At first, I must confess, I thought that this charming and intelligent lady had offered to work for us, especially as she refused our pay, in order to get information of the regiments and the prevailing diseases and sick rate of our army. Soon I had reason to know that she played the game, and stayed only in order to work to help the prisoners of her own people, and our wounded too. For any day her husband might want help from us or might be brought in wounded to our hospital, where she could nurse and tend to him herself. Our men liked to be attended by her, for she was gentler far than I and never short-tempered with them.

Nazoro we found in chains on our arrival for the offence of having attacked a German, and only his usefulness in the operating theatre saved him from the prison. In spite of the disapproval of Elizabeth and other Germans, I struck off the chains, feeling that he very probably had good excuse for his offence. But the Germans never failed to point out what a dangerous man he was. Once indeed he was slack and casual, so I promptly ordered him to be "kibokoed," and thereafter I could find no fault in his work and behaviour. Possessed of three wives, for he was passing rich on sixteen rupees a month, he asked one day for leave to celebrate the arrival of his first son. This I granted, only to be assailed a fortnight later by requests for leave to attend his grandmother's funeral, and to see a sick friend. But these had a familiar ring about them, and were not successful in procuring the lazy day that is so beloved by African humanity.

But Ali was of a different mould; small and slight and anxious to please, he was nevertheless swift to leave his work when once my back was turned. Forsaken in love--for he had been deserted by his wife--he had forsworn the sex and buried his sorrows in "Pombe," the Kaffir beer that effectually deprived him of what little intelligence he had. He was a "fundi" at taking out jiggers, and sat for hours at the feet of our foot-soldiers; quickly adopting an air of authority that occasionally brought him swift blows from East African troopers, who do not tolerate easily such airs in a native, he produced the unbroken jigger flea with unfailing regularity and prescribed the pail of disinfectant in which the tortured feet were soaked. Another long suit of his was the bandage machine, and the hours he could steal away from real work were spent in endless windings of washed though much stained bandages.

The German women hated us far more even than did the men; nor did those who, like Elizabeth, knew England, fail to believe any the less the German stories of English wickedness. When I told her of Portugal's entry into the war, and how our ancient and hereditary ally had handed over to England sixty out of the seventy-one German ships she had taken in her ports, Elizabeth snorted with rage and said that England, of course, forced all the little nations to fight against Germany.

One of my friends, and not the least welcome, was Corporal Nel. A Boer, he had come up from the Union with Brits. Tiring of war, he chose the nobler part played by the guard that cherishes German captured cattle. Swiftly losing his job owing to an outbreak of East Coast fever among his herd, he took to a vagabond's life. Wanted by the police in the Union, I am told, he avoided his regiment and lived with the natives. Forced to come to me one night with an attack of angina pectoris, he was grateful for the ease from suffering that amyl-nitrite, morphia and brandy gave in that exquisitely painful affliction. Accordingly he consented to organise some natives who should be armed with passes signed by me, and illuminated with Red Crosses and other impressive signs, and collect eggs and chickens and fruit for my patients in hospital. So impressed were the natives with the Ju-Ju conferred by my illumination of these passes with coloured chalks, that they brought me a daily and most welcome supply of these necessaries for our men. But the arm of the Law is long, and it sought out Corporal Nel within the native hut in which he made his home. And soon, to my sorrow and the infinite grief of our lambs in hospital, for whom those eggs, chickens, mangoes, and bananas spelt so much in the way of change of food, the Provost Sergeant had this wanderer in his chitches.

THE GERMAN IN PEACE AND WAR

"What do I think of this country, and how does the Hun of East Africa compare with his European brother?" you ask me. Well, to begin with the Colony, as of the greater importance, I must confess to be very taken with it, and I hope most sincerely that our Government will never give it back. Though it is not so suited as British East Africa for European colonisation, there are yet great areas of sufficient elevation to allow of white women and children living, for years, without suffering much from the vertical sun and the fevers of the country. There are many places where one only sees a mosquito for three months of the year, the soil is very fertile, and labour not only willing and efficient, but also very cheap. The European, too, has learnt to live properly in this country, and to avoid the midday sun; all offices and works are closed from twelve to three. If only man would learn wisdom in the amount of beer he drinks, and the food he eats, the tale of disease would be much less.

The colony is fully developed with excellent railways, well-built houses, a tractable and well-disciplined native population. Dar-es-Salaam in particular, seems to have been the apple of the German colonial eye. There are fine mission stations in all the healthy regions of the country, and great plantations of rubber, sisal, cotton, and corn abound. The white women and children, though rather pasty and washed out after at least two years' residence in the country, do not appear debilitated after their long tropical sojourn. The planters have, as a rule, invested all their belongings in their plantations, and make the country more a home than our people in East Africa, who are of a more wealthy and leisured class. Roads have been made and bridges built. In fact, the pioneering and donkey work has all been done, and the country only waits for us to step into our new inheritance.

To me it has been a source of surprise that the German, who consistently drinks beer in huge quantities, takes little or no exercise, and cohabits with the black women of the country extensively, should have performed such prodigies of endurance on trek in this campaign. One would have thought that the Englishman, who keeps his body fitter for games, eschews beer for his liver's sake, and finds that intimacy with the native population lowers his prestige, would have done far better in this war than the German. That in all fairness he has not done so is due to the fact that we, as an invading army, were unable to look after ourselves or to care for ourselves in the same way as the German.

We have had to carry kit and heavy ammunition, to sleep with only a ground sheet beneath us, through the tropic rains, to do without the shelter and protection of mosquito nets. The German soldier, even a private in a white or Schutzen Kompanie, as distinct from the under-officer with an Askari regiment or Feld Kompanie, as it is called, has had at least eight porters to carry all his kit, his food, his bed, to have his food ready prepared at the halting-places, and his bed erected, and mosquito curtains hung. Only on night patrols has he run risk from the mosquito. "How can you ask your men to carry loads and then fight as well, in Equatorial Africa?" they say to us. His captured chop boxes, for each individual is a separate unit and has his own food carried and prepared for him, have provided us, often, with the only square meals our men have enjoyed. Never short of food or drink or porters, ever marching toward his food supplies along a predetermined line of retreat, the German walks toward his dinner, as our men have marched away from theirs. Well paid too, five rupees a day pay and three rupees a day ration money, he had had no stint of eggs and chickens and the fruit of the country, that have been rarest of luxuries to us. "Far better if you had had fewer men and done them properly in the matter of food and hospitals and porters," captured German officers have often said to me. "How your men can stand it and do such marches is incredible to us." That is always the tenour of their remarks, their criticism, and they are clearly right, had such a policy been a practicable one for us, which it was not. At first the feeling between the soldiers of the two countries was good and war was conducted, even by them, in a more or less chivalrous manner. We thought the East African Hun a better fellow than his European brother. But it was only because he knew the game was up in East Africa, and thought that he had better behave properly, lest the retribution, that would be sure to follow, would fall heavily upon him. Later we found him to be the same old Hun, the identical savage that we know in Europe; the fear of consequences only restrains him here. It is his nature and the teaching of his schools and professors.

We have often been amazed at the disclosures from German officers' pocket-books. In the same oiled silk wrapping we find photographs of his wife and children, and cheek by jowl with them, the photographs of abandoned women and filthy pictures, such as can be bought in low quarters of big European cities. Their absence of taste in these matters has been incomprehensible to us. When we have taxed them with it, they are unashamed. "It is you who are hypocrites," they reply; "you like looking at forbidden pictures, if no one is about to see, but you don't carry them in your pocket-books. We, however, are natural, we like to look at such things, why should we not carry them with us?" If this be hypocrisy, I prefer the company of hypocrites. In their houses it was the same; disgusting pictures, masquerading in the guise of art, adorned the walls, evidences of corrupt taste and doubtful practices in every drawer and cupboard. Even the Commandant of Bukoba, von Stuemer, and his name did not belie his nature, though, before the war, quite popular with the British officials and planters of Uganda, had a queer taste in photography. In the big family album were evidences of his astonishing domestic life; for there were photographs of him in full regimentals, with medals and decorations, sitting on a sofa beside his wife, who was in a state of nature. Others portrayed him without the conventionalities of clothing, and his wife in evening dress.

Officers from the Cameroon have confirmed the filthy habits of the Huns and Hunnesses, how they defiled the rooms in the hospital at Duala that they occupied just before they were sent away; how disgusting were their habits in the cabins of the fine Atlantic liner that took them back to Europe. Not that it is their normal custom; it was merely to render the rooms uninhabitable for us who were to follow, and their special way of showing contempt and hatred for their foes. Do you wonder that the stewards and crew of the Union Castle liner struck work rather than convey and look after these beasts on the voyage to Europe? Our French missionary padre tells me that it was just the same in Alsace. The incident at Zabern after the manoeuvres was entirely due to the disgust and indignation of the French people at the defiling of their beds and bedrooms by the German soldiers, who had been billeted upon them.

LOOTING

Looting, although you may not know it, is the natural impulse of primitive man. And in war we are very primitive. To take what does not belong to one is very natural when a man is persuaded that he can be absolved from the charge of theft by quoting military necessity. How surely in war one sheds the conventions of society! It has the attraction of buried treasure; the charm of getting something for nothing. But there are different ways or degrees of looting.

Now there were a few of us in German East Africa who had been in the Retreat from Mons and the subsequent advance to the Marne and beyond it to the Aisne. Indelibly engraved upon our minds were the pictures of French chateaux and farmhouses looted by the German troops in their advance and abandoned to us in their retreat. All along the countless roads the German transport had pressed, hurrying to the Aisne, were evidences of the loot of German officers and men. In roadside ditches, half buried in the late summer vegetation, were pictures and bronzes, china and statuary, the loot the German officer had chosen to adorn the walls of his ancestral Schloss. Marble figures leant drunkenly against the wayside hedges, big brass clocks strewed the ditches. Long before, of course, had the German rank and file been compelled to jettison their prizes, for the transport horses were nearly foundered and only officers' loot could be retained. Later, when the exhaustion of the horses was complete, and capture of the waggons seemed imminent, the regimental equipment and food supply, and, finally, the loot of high officers had to be abandoned. The whole story of that retreat was to be read in the discard by the roadside. The regimental butcher had clung to his meat and the implements of his trade until the last; and when we found the roads littered with carcases of oxen, sacks of pea flour and sausage machines, we knew that we would shortly find the General's loot beside the hedge.

In the houses, too, both the chateaux and the comfortable French farmhouses, we saw what manner of man the Hun could be in the matter of looting. Where the soldier could not loot he could not refrain from destroying. Floors were knee-deep in women's gear, household goods, private letters and all the treasures of French linen chests. Trampled by muddy German boots were the fine whiteness of French bed-linen. Nor had the German soldier refrained from the last exhibit of his " *Kultur*," but left filthy evidences of his bestial habits behind him to ensure that the bedrooms would be uninhabitable by us.

Remembering all these things we wondered how our men would behave now that the tables were turned and they in a position to loot the treasures of many German farms and plantation houses. Of course, divisional orders against looting and wanton destruction were very strict. Where houses were at the mercy of small patrols and bodies of our men under non-commissioned officers, far from the path of the main advancing army, the temptation to all must have been immense, and it speaks volumes for the natural goodness of our men and their ingrained sense of order that never in this whole country was looting done by any of our troops. True many houses were plundered, and there was a certain amount of wanton damage; but it was all done by the plundering native or by the Hun himself in his retreat.

For our calculating enemy left no stone unturned to deprive us of any of the useful booty of war. He deliberately destroyed and ravaged and burnt the property of his fellow-countrymen, and mentally determined to send in the claim for damage against us. A German will always complain and send in a bill of costs to us, when he is once assured of the protection of British troops.

Naturally, of course, we requisitioned and gave receipts for any article or property that might be of use to us for our hospitals or our supplies. In fact, our scrupulous regard for enemy property will probably result in very many fraudulent claims against our Government when the war is over. How easy to add mythical articles of great value to the list attested to by the signature of a British Staff officer. Who could blame a Hun when the British were such fools and forgery of receipts so easy?

But such was the regard we paid to German women and children that, if a house were occupied, we took nothing and disturbed nothing. A German farmhouse was an oasis of plenty amid a very hungry army. It made us sometimes wonder whether it was quite right to leave German ducks and fowls and sheep behind us, when we had to live on mealie meal and tough trek-ox. But the women were so terrified, at first, that we gave such farms a wide berth when scarcity of water did not force us to camp within the enclosures. Shortly, however, as is the German custom, these women would profit by their immunity and come to regimental headquarters that listened so patiently and courteously to the tale of pawpaws or mangoes--fruit that was really wild--vanished in the night. In no campaign, I dare swear, has so much respect been given to occupied houses, so much consideration to conquered people. The German Government paid this compliment to our army, that they left their women and children behind to our tender mercies.

At Handeni, ours being a Casualty Clearing Station, our equipment included 200 stretchers, with little hospital equipment, beyond the men's own blankets and their kit. No sooner did we come along and install ourselves in the abandoned German fort than the 5th South African Infantry were in action at Kangata to win 125 casualties. For us they were to nurse and keep until convalescent; for there was no stationary hospital behind us, and forty miles of the worst of bad roads robbed us of the chance of transporting them to the railway.

So every afternoon I went to German planters' houses (empty, of course), for forty miles around, in a swift Ford car. And back in triumph we bore bedsteads and soft mattresses that heavy German bodies so lately had impressed. Warm from the Hun, we brought them to our wounded. Down pillows, soft eiderdown quilts for painful broken legs; mattresses for pain-racked bodies. And one's reward the pleasure and appreciation our men showed at these attempts to ameliorate *their* lot. They were so "bucked" to see us coming back at night laden with the treasures of German linen chests. It would have done your heart good to see their dirty, unwashed faces grinning at me from lace-edged pillows. Silk-covered cushions from Hun drawing-rooms for painful amputation stumps!

So I had the double pleasure, all the expectancy and the delight of seeing our men so pleased. Forty bedsteads and beds complete we found in that district, until the bare white-washed walls of the jail were transformed. White paint, too, we discovered in plenty, and soon our wards were virginal in their whiteness. And when I tell you that at one time I had no less than thirteen gunshot fractures of thigh and leg alone and other wounds in proportion, in the hospital, you may judge how necessary beds were.

But the natives had nearly always been before us, and the confusion was indescribable, drawers turned out, the contents strewed upon the floors, cupboards broken into, and all portable articles removed. Pathetic traces everywhere of the happy family life before war's devastating fingers rifled all their treasures. Photographs, private letters, a doll's house, children's broken toys.

And from some letters one gathered that insight into the relations between the plantation owner and the manager who lived there. At one farm, apparently owned by an Englishman who paid his manager, a German Dane from Flensburg, the princely sum of 200 rupees a month, we found that one, at least, of our own people knew how to grind the uttermost labour from his German employee. For there were letters from the manager asking for leave after 2 1/2 years' labour at this plantation, and pointing out that the German Government had laid down the principle of European leave every two years. To this came the cold reply that his employer cared nothing for German Government regulations; the contract was for three years, and he would see to it that this provision was carried out. One later letter begged for financial assistance to tide him over the coming months; for his wife and children had been ill and he himself in hospital at Korogwe with blackwater fever for two months. "And how shall I pay for food the next two months, if my pay is 200 rupees only, and hospital expenses 500?"

SHERRY AND BITTERS

A common inquiry put to doctors is, "What do you think of the alcohol question in a tropical campaign?" Do we not think that it is a good thing that our army is, by force of circumstances, a teetotal one? Much as we regret to depart from an attitude that is on the whole hostile to alcohol, I must say that it is our conviction that in the tropics a certain amount of diffusible stimulant is very beneficial and quite free from harm. And the cheapest and most reliable stimulant of that nature one can obtain commercially is, of course, whiskey. This whole campaign has been almost entirely a teetotal one for reasons of transport and inability to get drink. Not for any other reason, I can assure you. But where the absence of alcohol has been no doubt responsible for a wonderful degree of excellent behaviour among our troops, I yet know that the few who were able to get a drink at night felt all the better for it. At the end of the day here, when the sun has set and darkness, swiftly falling, sends us to our tents and bivouacs, there comes a feeling of intense exhaustion, especially if any exercise has been taken. And exercise in some form, as you have heard, is absolutely essential to health after the sun has descended toward the west about four o'clock in the afternoon. For men and officers go sick in standing camp more than on trek, and, often, the more and the longer the men are left in camp to rest, with the intention of recuperation, the more they go down with malaria and dysentery.

It is no sudden conclusion we have come to as to the value of alcohol, but we certainly feel that a drink or two at night does no one any harm. But the drink for tropics must not be fermented liquor: beer and wine are headachy and livery things. Whisky and particularly vermouth are far the best. And vermouth is really such a pleasant wholesome drink too. The idea of vermouth alone is attractive. For it is made from the dried flowers of camomile to which the later pressings of the grape have been added. One has only to smell dried camomile flowers to find that their fragrance is that of hay meadows in an English June! Camomile preparations, too, are now so largely used in medicine and still keep their reputation for wholesome and soothing qualities that it has enjoyed for generations. How could one think that harm could lurk in the tincture of such fragrant things as the flowers of English meadows? No little reputation as a cure and preventive for blackwater fever does vermouth enjoy! We know that we must always, if we would be wise, be guided by local experience and local custom, and it is told of the Anglo-German boundary Commission in East Africa, that the frontier between the two protectorates can still be traced by the empty vermouth bottles! But there were no cases of blackwater, I am told, on that very long and trying expedition.

In the survey of the whole question of Prohibition in the future, the essential difference of the requirements of humanity in tropical countries must be taken into consideration. There is no doubt, and in this all medical men of long tropical experience will agree, that some stimulant is needed by blond humanity living out of his geographical environment and debilitated by the adverse influence of his lack of pigment, the vertical sun and a tropical heat. It is more than probable that a proviso will have to be added to any world-wide scheme of prohibition. The cocktail, the universal "sherry and bitters" and "sundowner" will have to be retained. To expect a man, so exhausted that the very idea of food is distasteful, to digest his dinner, is to ask too much of one's digestive apparatus. And this we must all admit, that if a man in the tropics does not eat, then certainty he may not live.

NATIVE PORTERS

Toiling behind the column on march is the long and ragged line of native porters, the human cattle that are, after all, the most reliable form of transport in Equatorial Africa. Clad in red blankets or loin cloths or in kilts made of reeds and straw, they struggle on singing through the heat. Grass rings temper the weight of the loads to their heads, each man carrying his forty pounds for the regulation ten miles, the prescribed day's march in the tropics. Winding snake-like along the native paths, they go chanting a weird refrain that keeps their interest and makes the miles slip by. Here are some low-browed and primitive porters from the mountains, "Shenzies," as the superior Swahili call them, and clad only in the native kilt of grass or reeds. Good porters these, though ugly in form, and lacking the grace of the Wanyamwezi or the Wahehe.

At night they drop their loads beside the water-holes that mark the stages in the long march, and seek the nearest derelict ox or horse and prepare their meals, with relish, from the still warm entrails. This, with their "pocha," the allowance of mealie meal or mahoga, keeps them fat, their stomachs distended, bodies shiny and spirits of the highest. Round their camp fires they chatter far into the night, relieved, by the number of the troops and the plentiful supply of dead horses in the bush, from the ever-present fear of the lion that, in other days, would lift them at night, yelling, from their dying fires. One wonders that their spirits are so high, for they would get short shrift and little mercy from German raiding parties behind our advance. For the porter is fan-game, and is as liable to destruction as any other means of transport. Nor would the Germans hesitate a moment to kill them as they would our horses. But the bush is the porters' safeguard, and at the first scattering volley of the raiding party, they drop their loads and plunge into the undergrowth. Later, when we have driven off the raiders, it is often most difficult to collect the porters again. Naturally the British attitude to the porter *genus* differs from that of the Hun. Our aim, indeed, is to break up an enemy convoy, but we seek to capture the hostile porters that we may use them in our turn, all the more welcome to us for the increased usefulness that German porter discipline has given them.

Porters are the sole means of transport of the German armies; to these latter are denied the mule transport and the motor lorries that eat up the miles when roads are good. So they take infinite pains to train their beasts of burden. Often they are chained together in little groups to prevent them discarding their loads and plunging into the jungle when our pursuit draws near. The German knows the value of song to help the weary miles to pass, and makes the porters chant the songs and choruses dear to the native heart. Increasingly important these carriers become as the rains draw near, and the time approaches when no wheels can move in the soft wet cotton soil of the roads. Nor are the porters altogether easy to deal with. Very delicate they often are when moved from their own district and deprived of their accustomed food. Dysentery plays havoc in their ranks. For the banana-eating Baganda find the rough grain flour much too coarse and irritating for their stomachs. So our great endeavour is to get the greatest supply of local labour. Strange to say, it is here that our misplaced leniency to the German meets its due reward.

It is not easy to tell the combatant, unless he be caught red-handed. They all wear khaki, the only difference being that a civilian wears pearl buttons, the soldiers the metal military button with the Imperial Crown stamped on it. When it is borne in mind that the buttons are hooked on, one can imagine how simple it is to transform and change identity. Nor are the helmets different in any way, save that a soldier's bears the coloured button in the front; but as this also unscrews, the recognition is still more difficult.

With these people, it has been our habit to send them back to their alleged civil occupations after extracting an undertaking that they will take no further active or passive part in the war. But, to our surprise, when we sought for labour or supplies in their country districts, we found that we could obtain neither. Upon inquiry of the natives we learn that our late prisoners are conducting a campaign of intimidation. "Soon--in a year--we shall all return, and the English will be driven out. If you labour or sell eggs, woe betide you in the day of reckoning." What can the native do? As they say to us, "We see the Germans returning to their farms just as they were before; the missionaries installed in their mission stations again. What are we to believe?"

THE PADRE AND HIS JOB

How often, in this war, has not one pitied the Army Chaplain! As a visitor to hospital, as a dispenser of charity, as the bearer of hospital comforts and gifts to sick men, as an indefatigable organiser of concerts, as the cheerful friend of lonely men, he is doing a real good work. But that is not his job, it is not what he came out to do.

And the padre, willing, earnest, good fellow that he is, is conscious that he is often up against a brick wall, a reserve in the soldier that he cannot penetrate. The fact is, that he has rank, and that robs him of much of his power to reach the private soldier. But he must have rank, just as much as a doctor. Executive authority must be his, in order to assert and keep up discipline. And yet there is the constant barrier between the officer and the man. Doctors know and feel it: feel that, in the officer, they are no longer the doctor. Now, however, great changes have been wrought and the medical officer likes to be called "doc," just as much as the chaplain values the name "padre." There's something so intimate about it. Such a tribute to our job and our responsibility and the trust and confidence they have in us.

The soldier is not concerned about his latter end; all that troubles him about his future, is the billet he yearns for, the food he hopes to get, the rest he is sure is due to him, his leave and the time when--how he longs for that!--he may turn his sword into a ploughshare and have done with war and the soldier's beastly trade.

Of course, in little matters like swearing, the padre is wise and he knows what Tommy's adjective is worth. He knows that Tommy is a simple person and apt to reduce his vocabulary to three wonderful words: three adjectives which are impartially used as substantives, adjectives, verbs, or adverbs. That is all. The earnest young chaplain at first gasps with horror at the flaming words, and would not be surprised if the heavens opened and celestial wrath descended on these poor sinners' heads. But he soon learns that these little adornments of the King's English mean less than nothing. For Tommy is a reverent person, he is not a blasphemer in reality; he is gentle, infinitely kind, incredibly patient, extraordinarily generous, if the truth be told. His language would lead one to believe that his soul is entirely lost. But when one knows what this careless, generous, and kindly person is capable of, one feels that his soul is a very precious thing indeed. And there is one way the padre can touch this priceless soul: that is, by serving in the ranks with him. Then all the barriers fall, all the reserve vanishes, and the padre comes into his own, and saves more souls by his example than by oceans of precept. There he finds himself, he has got his real job at last.

Among the South African infantry brigade, that did that wonderful march to Kondoa Irangi, two hundred and fifty miles in a month, in the height of the rainy season, were fourteen parsons. All serving in the ranks as private soldiers, they carried a wonderful example with them. It was their pride that they were the cleanest and the best disciplined men in their respective companies. No fatigue too hard, no duty too irksome. Better soldiers they showed themselves than Tommy himself. Of a bright and cheerful countenance, particularly when things looked gloomy, they were ready for any voluntary fatigue. The patrol in the thick bush that was so dangerous, fetching water, quick to build fires and make tea, ready to help a lame fellow with his equipment, always cheery, never grousing, they lived the life of our Lord instead of preaching about it.

For the padre's job, I take it, is to teach the men the right spirit, to send them to war as men should go, to assure them that this is a holy fight, that God is on their side.

He knows that Tommy, if he speculates at all upon his latter end, does so in the pagan spirit, the spirit that teaches men that there is a special heaven for soldiers who are killed in war, that the manner of their dying will give them absolution for their sins. And the padre knows that the pagan spirit is the true spirit and yet he may not say so. He may not suggest for a moment that sin will be forgiven by sacrifice, for that is Old Testament teaching; his Bishop tells him that he must not trifle with this heresy, but he must inculcate in sinful man that he can, by repentance, and by repentance only, gain absolution for past misdeeds.

And the chaplain knows Tommy, and he knows that he will never get him on that tack. He knows that any soldier, who is any good, looks upon it as a cowardly, mean and contemptible thing to crawl to God for forgiveness in times of danger, when they never went to him in days of peace. And I know many a chaplain who is with the soldier in this belief.

A little of war, and the padre very soon finds his limitations. To begin with, he is attached to a Field Ambulance and not to a regiment, as a rule. The only time he sees the men is when they are wounded. Then he often feels in the way and fears to obstruct the doctor in his job. So all that is left is going out with the stretcher-bearing party at night, showing a good example, cool in danger, merciful to the wounded. But that again is not his job.

First, when he laid aside the sad raiment of his calling, and put on his khaki habiliments of war, he thought that the chief part of his job was to shrive the soldier before action, and to comfort the dying. Later he found that the soldier would not be shriven, and found, to his surprise, that the dying need no comfort. Very soon he learnt that wounded men want the doctor, and chiefly as the instrument that brings them morphia and ease from pain. And when the wound is mortal, God's mercy descends upon the man and washes out his pain. How should he need the padre, when God Himself is near?

Early in his military career the young ministers of the Gospel were provided with small diaries, in which they might record the dying messages of the wounded. Then came disillusion, and they found the dying had no messages to send; they are at peace, the wonderful peace that precedes the final dissolution, and all they ask is to be left alone.

So is it to be wondered at, that men with imagination, men like Furze, the Bishop of Pretoria, saw in a vision clear that the padre's job lay with the living and not with the dying, that he could point the way by the example of a splendid life with the soldier, far better than by a hundred discourses, as an officer, from the far detachment of the pulpit. Thus was the idea conceived and so was the experiment carried out. And all of us who were in German East Africa can vouch for the splendid results of these excellent examples. For the private soldier saw that his fellow-soldier, handicapped as he was by being a parson, could know his job and do his job as a soldier better than Tommy could himself. To his surprise, he found that here was a man who could make himself intelligible without prefixing a flaming adjective when he asked his pal to pass the jam. Here was a N.C.O., a real good fellow too, who could give an order and point a moral without the use of a blistering oath; a man who was a man, cool under fire, ready for any dangerous venture, cheerful always, never grousing, always generous and open as a soldier should be, never preaching, never openly praying, never asking men to do what he would not do himself. Can you wonder that Tommy understood, and, understanding, copied this example?

When he saw a man inspired by some inward Spirit that made him careless of danger, contemptuous of death, fulfilling all the Soldier's requirements in the way of manhood, he knew quite well that some Divine inward fire upheld this once despised follower of Christ. Then lo! the transformation. First, the oaths grew rarer in the ranks and vanished; then came the discovery that, after all, it really was possible to conduct a conversation in the same language as the soldier used at home with his wife and children; that, after all, the picturesque adjectives that flavoured the speech of camps were not necessary; that there was really no need for two kinds of speech, the language of the camp and the language of the drawing-room.

And the process of redemption was very curious. All are familiar of course with the hymn tunes that are sung by marching soldiers, tunes that move their female relatives and amiable elderly gentlemen to a quick admiration for the Christian soldier. All know too that, could the admiring throng only hear the words to which these hymn tunes were sung, the crowd would fly with fingers to their ears, from such apparent blasphemy. Well, these well-known ballads were first sung at the padre, and especially at the padre who was masquerading as a soldier. And when the soldier saw that the padre could see the jest and laugh at it too, and know that it meant nothing, then he felt that he had got a good fellow for his sky pilot. Can you wonder that the soldier spoke of his padre comrade in such generous terms and that the whole tone of the regiment improved? The men were better soldiers and better Christians too.

There is one trap into which a padre falls when marching with a regiment. Provided, by regulations, with a horse, he is often unwise enough to ride alongside his marching cure of souls. It would, perhaps, do him good if he could hear, as I did, the comments of two Scottish sergeants in the rear. "Our Lord did not consider it beneath him to ride upon a donkey, but this man of God needs must have a horse."

"How is it that I don't get close to the good fellows on board the ship?" said a very good and earnest padre to me. "Why don't these fellow-officers of mine come to church? How is it that fellows I know to be good and generous and kindly are yet to be found at the bar, in the smoking-room, when my service is on? Why is it that the decent, nice fellows aren't professing Christians, and some of the fellows who are my most regular attendants haven't a tenth of the character and quality and charm of these apparent pagans?"

What could I do but tell him the truth? I knew him well and felt that he would understand. Most fellows, I said, don't come to church, because if they've good and decent characters, they hate to be hypocrites. Now you know, padre, in this improper world of ours, that many men are sinners, by that I mean that convention describes as sinful some of the things they do. What do you tell us when we go to early chapel in the morning? "Ye that do truly and earnestly repent you of your sins and are in love and charity with your neighbours and intend to lead a new life ... draw near with faith and take this Holy Sacrament ..." Well, then, can you conceive that such a state of mind exists in an otherwise decent man that he finds the burden of his sin not intolerable, as he should do, but that he hugs that special sin as a prisoner may hug his chains? That his sin, or let us call it his breach of the conventions of Society, is the one dear precious thing in his existence at the present moment. He doesn't want to reform or to lead a new life. Later, no doubt, he'll tire of this sin and then he may come to church again. But how could a man of character go to God's House and be such an infernal hypocrite? He cannot partake of the Body and Blood of Christ any more when he is in that state of mind. So you see, padre, it is often the honest men who won't be hypocrites, that won't go to your church.

Many the padre that used to drift into our hospital on the long trek to Morogoro, Church of England, Roman Catholics, Presbyterians, and those who look after the "fancy religions," as Tommy calls them. By that term is designated any man who does not belong to either of the above three. One such fellow came to our mess the other day, and in answer to our query as to the special nature of his flock, he answered that, though strictly speaking a Congregationalist, he had found that he had become a "dealer in out-sizes in souls," as he called it. He kept, as he said, a fatherly eye (and a very good eye too, that we could see) on Dissenters in general, Welsh Baptists, Rationalists, and all the company of queerly minded men we have in this strange army of ours. Later we heard that he had brought with him an excellent reputation from the Front. And that is not easy to acquire from an army that is hard to please in the matter of professors of religion.

FOR ALL PRISONERS AND CAPTIVES

The missionaries and the Allied civilians released from Tabora have the usual tale to tell of German beastliness, of white men forced to dig roads and gardens, wheel barrows and other degrading work under the guard of native soldiers, insulted, humiliated, degraded before the native Askaris at the instance of German officers and N.C.O.s in charge. The Italian Consul-General working in the roads! We may forget all this: it is in keeping with our soft and sentimental ways. But will the French? Will Italy forgive? There will be no weakness there when the day of reckoning comes. All this we had from the Commission of Inquiry in Morogoro and Mombasa that sat to take evidence. Gentle nurses of the Universities' English Mission, missionary ladies who devoted a lifetime in the service of the Huns and the natives in German East, locked up behind barbed wire for two years, without privacy of any kind, constantly spied upon in their huts at night by the native guard, always in terror that the black man, now unrestrained, even encouraged by his German master, should do his worst. Can you wonder that they kept their poison tablets for ever in their pockets that they might have close at hand an end that was merciful indeed compared with what they would suffer at native hands? So with many tears of relief they cast friendly Death into the bushes as the Askaris fled before the dust of our approaching columns. Do you blame gentle Sister Mabel that she would never speak to any Hun in German, using only Swahili and precious little of that?

Far worse the story told by the broken Indian soldiers, prisoners since the fight at Jassin, left abandoned, half dead with dysentery and fever, by the Germans on their retreat to Mahenge. A commission of inquiry held by British officers of Native Indian regiments elicited the facts. The remains of two double companies, one Kashmiris, the other Bombay Grenadiers, to the number of 150, were brought to Morogoro and there farmed out to German contractors. Here they toiled on the railway, clearing the land, bringing in wood from the jungle building roads, half starved and savagely ill-treated. They might burn with fever or waste their feeble strength in dysentery, it made no difference to their brutal jailers. To be sick was to malinger in German eyes: so they got "Kiboko" and their rations reduced, because, forsooth, a man who could not work could also not eat. To "Kiboko" a prisoner of war and an Indian soldier is a flagrant offence against the laws of war. But to the contractor there were no laws but of his making, and he laid on thirty lashes with the rhinoceros hide Kiboko to teach these stiff-necked "coolies" not to sham again. And as these soldiers lay half dead with fever on the road, their German jailers gave orders that their mouths and faces be defiled with filth, a crime unspeakable to a Moslem. Will the Mohammedan world condone this? The fruit of this treatment was that eighty of these wretched soldiers died and were buried at Morogoro. But these prisoners, on their release, marching through the streets caught sight of two of their erstwhile jailers walking in freedom and security and going about then daily avocations as if there was no war. These Germans had, of course, told our Provost Marshal that they were civilians, and never had or intended to take part in the war. So these two men on their word, the word of a Prussian, mark you well, were allowed all the privileges of freedom in Morogoro. One of them, Dorn by name, a hangdog ruffian, owned the house we took over as a mess, and tried to get receipts from us for things we took for the hospital, that really belonged to other people.

But the Indian soldiers' evidence was the undoing of Dorn and his fellow-criminal. Arrested and put into jail, they were sent to Dar-es-Salaam for trial by court-martial on the evidence. How the guard hoped that an attempt to escape would be made, such an attempt as was so often the alleged reason for the shooting of so many of our English prisoners. The sense of discipline in the Indian troops was such that, no matter how great the temptation to avenge a thousand injuries and the unexampled opportunity offered by a long railway journey through dense bush, they delivered their prisoners safe in Dar-es-Salaam. It is said that nothing would persuade Dorn and his comrade to leave the safe shelter of the railway truck. No, they did not want to go for a walk in the bush, they would stay in the truck, thank you! No matter how great the invitation to flight was offered by an open door and the temporary disappearance of the guard. Do you think these two ruffians will get the rope? I wonder.

The other day at Kissaki the Germans sent back ten of our white prisoners, infantry captured at Salaita Hill, Marines from the *Goliath*. All these weary months the Huns had dragged these wretched prisoners all over the country. And yet there are some who tell us that the German is not such a Hun here as he is in Europe. The fact is he is worse, if possible, inconceivably arrogant and cruel at first, incredibly anxious to conciliate our prisoners when the tide had turned and vengeance was upon him. Burning by fever by day, chilled by tropic dews at night, these poor devils had been harried and kicked and cursed and ill-used by Askaris and insulted by native porters all that long retreat from Moschi to Kissaki and beyond. No "machelas" for them if they were ill, no native hammocks to carry them on when their poor brains cried out against the malaria that struck them down in the noonday sun. Kicked along the road or left to die in the bush, these the only two alternatives. And the beasts were kinder than the Huns: they at least took not so long to kill. Forced to do coolie labour, to dig latrines for native soldiers, incredibly humiliating, such was their lot! Many of them died by the roadside. Many died for want of medicine. There was no lack of drugs for Germans, but there was need for economy where prisoners were concerned. What more natural than that they should keep their drugs for their own troops? Who could tell their pressing need in months to come? But the indomitable ones they kept and keep them still. Only yesterday they released the naval surgeon captured on the pseudo-hospital ship *Tabora* in Dar-es-Salaam. Did he get the treatment that custom ordains an officer should have, or did he also dig latrines and cook his *bit* of dripping meat over a wood fire like a "shenzy" native? I leave that to you to answer. How could we tell he was a doctor? that is the Huns' excuse. "He only had a blue and red epaulet on his white drill tunic, there was no red cross on his arm." But apparently after twenty months they discovered this essential fact. And what was left of him struggled into our lines under a white flag the other day. But here, as in Germany, not all the Huns were Hunnish. Some there were who cursed Lettow and the war in speaking to the prisoners, and, in private talks, professed their tiredness of the whole beastly campaign. But these, our men noticed, were ever the quickest to "strafe," always the first to rail and upbraid and strike when a German officer was near.

Fed on native food, chewing manioc, mahoja for their flour, the ground their bed, so they existed; but ever in their captive hearts was the knowledge that we were coming on, behind them ever the thunder of our guns, the panic flights of their captors, timid advances from native soldiers, unabashed tokens of conciliation from the Europeans alternating with savage punishment. This was meat and drink indeed to them. Cheerfully they endured, for Nemesis was at hand. How they chuckled to see the German officer's heavy kit cut down to one chop box, native orderlies cut off, fat German doctors waddling and sweating along the road? Away and ever away to the south, for the hated "Beefs" were after them, coming down relentlessly from the north. Even a lay brother, "Brother John," they kept until the other day. And their stiff-necked prisoners refused to receive the conciliatory amelioration of their lot that would be offered one day, to be, for no apparent reason, withdrawn the next. "No, thank you, we don't want extra food now! We really don't need a native servant now, we will still do our own fatigues. No. We don't want to go for a walk. We've really been without all these things for so long that we don't miss them now. Anyhow it won't be for long," they said.

The German commandant turned away furiously after the rejection of his olive branch. For he knew now that his captives knew that the game was up, and it gave him food for thought indeed.

THE BEASTS OF THE FIELD

We are camped for the present on the edge of a plateau, overlooking a vast plain that stretches a hundred miles or more to where Kilimanjaro lifts his snow peaks to the blue. All over this yellow expanse of grass, relieved in places by patches of dark bush, are great herds of wild game slowly moving as they graze. Antelope and wildebeests, zebra and hartebeests, there seems no end to them in this sportsman's paradise. At night, attracted by to-morrow's meat that hangs inside a strong and well-guarded hut, the hyaenas come to prowl and voice their hunger and disappointment on the evening air.

The general impression in England, you know, was that in coming to East Africa we had left the cold and damp misery of Flanders for a most enjoyable side-show. We were told that we should spend halcyon days among the preserves, return laden with honours and large stores of ivory, and in our spare moments enjoy a little campaigning of a picnic variety, against an enemy that only waited the excuse to make a graceful surrender. But how different the truth! To us with the advance there has been no shooting; to shoot a sable antelope (and, of course, we have trekked through the finest game preserves in the world, including the Crown Prince's special Elephant Forests) is to ask for trouble from the Askari patrol that is just waiting for the sound of a rifle shot to bring him hot foot after us. So the sable antelope might easily be bought by very unpleasant sacrifice. All shooting at game, even for food, except on most urgent occasions, is strictly forbidden, for a rifle shot may be as misleading to our own patrols and outposts as it would be inviting to the Hun.

This war had led us from the comparative civilisation of German plantations to the wildest, swampiest region of Equatorial Africa. After rain the roads tell the story of the wild game, for in the mud are the big slot marks of elephants and lions and all the denizens of the bush. But at the bases and back in British East Africa where there are no lurking German Askari patrols, many fellows have had the time of their lives with the big game. Afternoon excursions to the wide plains and their bush where the wild game hide and graze.

We are often asked how we manage to avoid the lions and the other wild beasts of the country that come to visit the thorn bomas that protect our transport cattle at night? Strange as it may seem, we do not have to avoid them, for they do not come for us or for the natives, nor yet for the live cattle so much as for the dead mules and oxen. I dare say there have never been so many white and black men in a country infested with lions who have suffered so little from the beasts of the field as we have.

In the first place, the advance of so great an army has frightened away a very large number of the wild game. All that have stayed are the larger carnivora, like the hyaena or the lion. And they are a positive Godsend to us. For instead of attacking our sentries and patrols at night, as you might imagine, they are the great scavengers and camp cleaners of the country. Of vultures there are too few in this land, probably because the blind bush robs them of the chance of spotting their prey. Were it not for lions and hyaenas, we should be in a bad way. For they come to eat all our dead animals, all the wastage of this army, the tribute our transport animals are paying to fly and to horse-sickness. For in spite of fairy tales about lions one must believe the unromantic truth that a lion prefers a dead ox to a man, and a black man to a white one. So you will not be surprised when I tell you that in this army of ours of at least 30,000 men I have only had two cases of mauling by the larger carnivora to deal with. And such cases as these would all pass through my hands. There was only one case of lion mauling, and that a Cape Boy who met a young half-grown cub on the road and unwisely ran from it. At first curiosity attracted this animal, and later the hunting instinct caused him to maul his prey. So they brought him in with the severe blood-poisoning that sets in in almost all cases of such a nature. For the teeth and claws of the larger carnivora are frightfully infectious. This Cape Boy died in forty-eight hours. Yet one other case was that of an officer who met a leopardess with cubs in the bush when out after guinea fowl. She charged him, and he gave her his left arm to chew to save his face and body. Then alarmed by his yells and the approach of his companion she left him, and he was brought one hundred miles to the railway. But he was in good hands at once, and when I saw him the danger of blood-poisoning had gone and he was well upon his way to health again.

The same experience have we had with snakes. The hot dry dusty roads and the torn scrub abound with snakes and most of them of a virulently poisonous quality. But one case only of snake-bite have I seen, and that a native. The fact that the wild denizens of the field and forest are much more afraid of us than we of them saves us from what might appear to be very serious menace. Even the wounded left out in the dense bush have not suffered from these animal pests, but the dead, of course, have often disappeared and their bleached bones alone are left to tell the story. One might think that the hyaena, the universal scavenger, would be as loathed by the native as he is by us whose dead he disinters at night, if we have been too tired or unable to bury our casualties deep enough. But, strange as it may seem, the hyaena is worshipped by one very large tribe in East Africa, the Kikuyu. For these strange people have an extraordinary aversion to touching dead people. So much so, that when their own relatives seem about to die they put them out in the bush with a small fire and a gourd of water, protected by a small erection of bush against the mid-day sun, and leave the hyaenas to do the rest. So it comes about that this beast is almost sacred, and a white man who kills one runs some danger of his life, if the crime is discovered. It is hardly to be wondered at that the hyaenas in the "Kikuyu" country are far bolder than in other parts. Elsewhere and by nature the hyaena is an arrant coward. Here, however, he will bite the face off a sleeping man lying in the open, or even pull down a woman or child, should they be alone; elsewhere he only lives on carrion.

The German is not a sportsman as we understand the term, though the modern young German who apes English ways, comes out to East Africa occasionally to make collections for his ancestral Schloss. That the Crown Prince should have re-served large areas for game preserves speaks for this modern tendency in young Ger-many. The average German is not keen on exercise in the tropics, he will be carried by sweating natives in a chair or hammock where Englishmen on similar errands will walk and shoot upon the way. This slothful habit leads us to the conviction that very much of the country is not explored as it should be, and I have been told by prospectors for precious minerals, who were serving in our army, of the wonder-ful store of mineral deposits in German East Africa. One noted prospector who fell into my hands at Handeni could so little forget his occupation of peace in this new reality of war, that he always took out his prospector's hammer on patrol with him, and chipped pieces of likely rock to bring back to camp in his haversack. He it was who told me of his discovery of a seam of anthracite coal in the bed of a river near the Tanga railway. On picket he had wandered to the edge of the ravine and fallen over. Struggling for life to save himself by the shrubs and growing plants on the face of this precipice, he eventually found his way to the bottom of the ravine, on the top of a small avalanche of earth. Judge, then, of his astonishment when, look-ing up, he saw that his fall had exposed a fine seam of coal. This discovery alone, in a country where the railway engines are forced to burn wood fuel or expensive imported coal from Durban, is of the greatest importance. The experience of most of us seemed to be that the Germans, in the piping days of peace, preferred elegant leisure in a hammock and the prospect of cold beer beneath a mango tree to the sterner delights of laborious days in thickly wooded and inaccessible mountains. One of the first results of this campaign will be to bring the enterprising prospector from Rhodesia and the Malay States to what was once the "Schoene Ost-Afrika" of the German colonial enthusiast.

But big game hunting, except a man hunts for a living, as do the elephant poachers in Mozambique or the Lado Enclave, soon loses its savour to white men after a time. It is not long before the rifle is discarded for the camera by men who really care for wild life in wilder countries. Herein the white man differs from the savage, who kills and kills until he can slay no longer. Strange it is to think that farmers and planters in East Africa so soon tire of big game hunting, that they do not trouble even to shoot for the pot or to get the meat that is the ration provided for their native labourers, but employs a native, armed with a rifle and a few cartridges, to shoot antelope for meat.

To one in whom the spirit of adventure and romance is not dead what more attractive than an elephant hunter's life? To work for six months and make two or three thousand pounds, and spend the proceeds in a riotous holiday, until the heavy tropic rains are over and the bush is dry again. But few realise the rare qualities that an elephant hunter must have. He must be extraordinarily tough, quite hardened to the toil and diseases of the country, knowing many native tongues, largely immune from the fever that lays a white man low many marches from civilisation and hospitals, of an endurance splendid, with hope to dare the risk, and courage to endure the toil. For the professional elephant hunter is now, by force of circumstance and white man's law, become a wolf of the forest, and the hands of all Governments are against him. He must mark his elephant down, be up with the first light and after him, must manoeuvre for light and wind and scent to pick the big bull from the sheltering herd of females. If the head shot is not possible, the lung shot or stomach shot alone is left. And six hours' march through waterless country before one comes up with the elephant resting with his herd is not the best preparation for a shot. If one misses, one may as well go home another eight hours back to water. But if you hit and follow the bull through the thorny bush, you do not even then know whether you will find the victim. If, however, you find traces three times in the first hour, or see the blood pouring from the trunk--not merely blown in spray upon the bushes--then the certain conviction comes that within an hour you will find your kill. Then the long march back to camp, all food and water and the precious tusks carried by natives, often too exhausted at the end to eat. A man who cannot march thirty miles a day, and fulfil all the other requirements, should relegate elephant hunting to the world of dreams. All the big successful elephant poachers are well known: most of them are English, some of them are Boers, a few only French or American; but seldom does a German attempt it or live to repeat his experience. Far better to shut his eyes to this illicit traffic and assist these strange soldiers of fortune to get their ivory to the coast, and then enjoy the due reward of this complaisant attitude.

THE BIRDS OF THE AIR

I think it is rather a pity that no naturalist has studied the birds of German East Africa in the intimate and friendly spirit that many men have done at home. It has been said that the bright plumage of Central African birds is given them as compensation for the charm of song that is a monopoly of the European bird. That this is the case in the damp forests and swamps and reed beds along the Rufigi and other big rivers, there is no doubt. Gaudy parrots and iridescent finches flash through the foliage of trees along the Mohoro river, monkeys slide down the ropes formed by parasitic plants that hang from the tree branches, to dip their hands in the water to drink; only to flee, chattering to the tree-tops, as they meet the gaze of apparently slumbering crocodiles. Great painted butterflies flit above the beds of lilies that fringe the muddy lagoons, the hippopotamus wallows lazily in the warm sunlit waters. Here, it is true, is the Equatorial Africa of our schoolboy dreams; and the birds have little but their glittering plumage to recommend them.

But we are apt to forget that the greater portion of Tropical Africa, certainly all that is over five hundred feet above the sea, which constitutes the greater part of the country with the exception of the coast region, is not at all true to the picture that most of us have in our minds. For the character of the interior is vastly different: great rolling plains of yellow grass and thorn scrub, with the denser foliage of deciduous trees along the river-banks. Here, indeed, you may find sad-coloured birds that are gifted with the sweetest of songs. In the bed of the Morogoro River lives a warbler who sings from the late afternoon until dusk, and he is one of the very few birds that have that deep contralto note, the "Jug" of the nightingale. And there are little wrens with drab bodies and crimson tails that live beside the dwellings of men and pick up crumbs from the doors of our tents, and hunt the rose trees for insects. In the thorn bushes of higher altitudes are grey finches that might have learnt their songs beside canary cages. The African swallows, red headed and red backed, have a most tuneful little song; they used to delight our wounded men in hospital at Handeni when they built their nests in the roofs of this one-time German jail, and sang to reward us for the open windows that allowed them to feed their broods of young.

In the mealie fields are francolins in coveys, very like the red-legged partridge in their call, though in plumage nearer to its English brother. There, too, the ubiquitous guinea fowl, the spotted "kanga" that has given us so many blessed changes of diet, utters his strident call from the tops of big thorn trees. The black and white meadow lark is here, but the "khoran" or lesser bustard of South Africa, that resembles him so much in plumage on a much larger scale, is absent. The brown bustard, so common in the south, is the only representative of the turkey tribe that I have seen here. Black and white is a very common bird colouring; black crows with white collars follow our camps and bivouacs to pick up scraps, and the brown fork-tailed kite hawks for garbage and for the friendly lizard too, in the hospital compound. One night, as I lay in my tent looking to the moon-lit camp, Fritz, our little ground squirrel that lived beneath the table of the mess tent, met an untimely fate from a big white owl. A whirr of soft owl wings to the ground outside my tent, a tiny squeak, and Fritz had vanished from our compound too.

Vultures of many kinds dispute with lion and hyaena for the carrion of dead ox or mule beside the road of our advance. King vultures in their splendour of black, bare red necks and tips of white upon their wings, lesser breeds of brown carrion hawks and vultures attend our every camp. Again the vulture is not so common as in South Africa, for here it is blind in this dense bush and has to play a very subsid-

iary part to the scavenging of lions and hyaenas. Down by the swamps one evening
we shot a vulture that was assisting a moribund ox to die. True we did not mean to
kill him, for we owe many debts of gratitude to vultures; but, to my surprise, my native boy seemed greatly pleased. Lifting the big black tail he showed me the white
soft feathers beneath, and by many signs appeared to indicate that these feathers
were of great value. Then I looked again, and it was a marabou stork. My boy, who
had been with marabou and egret poachers in the swamps and rice-fields of the
lower Rufigi, knew the value of these snowy feathers.

BITING FLIES

Of the many plagues that beset this land of Africa not the least are the biting
flies. Just as every tree and bush has thorns, so every fly has a sting. Some bite by
day only, some by night, and others at all times. Even the ants have wings, and drop
them in our soup as they resume their plantigrade existence once again.

The worst biter that we have met in the many "fly-belts" that lie along the
Northern Railway is the tsetse fly: especially was he to be found at a place called
Same, and during the long trek from German Bridge on the Northern Railway to
Morogoro in the south. At one place there is a belt thirty miles wide, and our progress was perpetual torture, unless we passed that way at night. For the *Glossina
morsitans* sleeps by night beneath leaves in the bush, and only wakes when disturbed. For this reason we drive our horses, mules, and cattle by night through
these fly-belts. Savage and pertinacious to a degree are these pests, and their bite is
like the piercing of a red-hot needle. Simple and innocent they appear, not unlike
a house fly, but larger and with the tips of their wings crossed and folded at the
end like a swallow's. They are mottled grey in colour, and their proboscis sticks
out straight in front. Hit them and they fall off, only to rise again and attack once
more; for their bodies are so tough and resistant, that great force is required to destroy them. They are infected with trypanosomes, a kind of attenuated worm that
circulates in the blood, but fortunately not the variety that causes sleeping sickness.
At least we believe not. In any case we shall not know for eighteen months, for that
is usually the latent period of sleeping sickness in man. Their bite is very poison-

ous, and frequently produces the most painful sores and abscesses. But if they are not lethal to man, they take a heavy toll of horses, mules, and cattle. Through the night watches, droves of horses, remounts for Brits's and Vandeventer's Brigades, cattle for our food and for the transport, mules and donkeys, pass this way. Fine sleek animals that have left the Union scarcely a month before, carefully washed in paraffin in a vain attempt to protect them from flies and ticks. But what a change in a short six weeks. The coat that was so sleek now is staring, the eye quite bloodless, the swelling below the stomach that tells its own story; wasting, incredible. Soon these poor beasts are discarded, and line the roads with dull eyes and heavy hanging heads. We may not shoot, for firing alarms our outposts and discloses our position. To-night the lions and hyaenas that this war has provided with such sumptuous repasts will ring down the curtain. A horse's scream in the bush at night, the lowing of a frightened steer, a rustling of bushes, and these poor derelicts, half eaten by the morning, meet the indifferent gaze of the next convoy. More merciful than man are the scavengers of the forest. They, at least, waste no time at the end. Strange that the little donkeys should alone for a time at least escape the fly; it is their soft thick coats that defeats the searching proboscis. But after rain or the fording of a river their protecting coats get parted by the moisture, and the fly can find his mark in the skin. So the donkey and the Somali mule that generations of fly have rendered tolerant to the trypanosome are the most reliable of our beasts of burden. Soon, these too will go in the approaching rainy season, and then we shall fall back on the one universal beast of burden, the native carriers. Thousands of these are now being collected to march with their head loads at the heels of our advancing columns. The veterinary service is helpless with fly-struck animals. One may say with truth that the commonest and most frequently prescribed veterinary medicine is the revolver. Certainly it is the most merciful. Large doses of arsenic may keep a fly-struck horse alive for months; alive, but robbed of all his life and fire, his free gait replaced by a shambling walk. The wild game, more especially the water buck and the buffalo whose blood is teeming with these trypanosomes, but who, from generations of infection, have acquired an immunity from these parasites, keep these flies infected. Thus one cannot have domestic cattle and wild game in the same area; the two are incompatible. And shortly the time will come, as certainly as this land will support a white population, when the wild game will be exterminated and *Glossina mor-*

sitans will bite no more.

More troublesome, because more widely spread, are the large family of mosquitoes. The **anopheles**, small, grey and quietly persistent, carries the malaria that has laid our army low. **Culex**, larger and more noisy, trumpets his presence in the night watches: but the mischief he causes is in inverse ratio to the noise he makes. **Stegomyia**, host of the spirium of yellow fever, is also here, but happily not yet infected; not yet, but it may be only a question of time before yellow fever is brought along the railways or caravan routes from the Congo or the rivers of the West Coast, where the disease is endemic. There for many years it was regarded as biliary fever or blackwater or malaria. Now that the truth is known a heavier responsibility is cast upon the already overburdened shoulders of the Sanitary Officer and the specialists in tropical diseases. **Stegomyia**, as yet uninfected, are also found in quantities in the East; and with the opening of the Panama Canal, that links the West Indies and Caribbean Sea, where yellow fever is endemic, with the teeming millions of China and India, may materially add to the burden of the doctors in the East. Living a bare fourteen days as he does, infected **stegomyia** died a natural death, in the old days, during the long voyage round the Horn, and thus failed to infect the Eastern Coolie, who would in turn infect these brothers of the West Indian mosquito.

Fortunate it is in one way that **anopheles** is the mosquito of lines of communication, of the bases, of houses and huts and dwellings of man, rather than of the bush. Our fighting troops are consequently not so exposed as troops on lines of communication. For this blessing we are grateful, for lines of communication troops can use mosquito nets, but divisional troops on trek or on patrol cannot. Soon we shall see the fighting troops line up each evening for the protective application of mosquito oil. For where nets are not usable it is yet possible to protect the face and hands for six hours, at least, by application of oil of citronella, camphor, and paraffin. Nor is this mixture unpleasant; for the smell of citronella is the fragrance of verbena from Shropshire gardens.

Least in size, but in its capacity for annoyance greatest, perhaps, of all, is the sand fly. Almost microscopic, but with delicate grey wings, of a shape that Titania's self might wear, they slip through the holes of mosquito gauze and torment our feet by night and day. The three-day fever they leave behind is yet as nothing compared to the itching fury that persists for days.

Finally there is the bott-fly, by no means the least unpleasant of the tribe. Red-headed and with an iridescent blue body, he is very similar to the bluebottle, and lives in huts and dwellings. But his ways are different, for he bites a hole into one's skin, usually the back or arms, and lays an egg therein. In about ten days this egg develops into a fully grown larva, in other words a white maggot with a black head. It looks for all the world like a boil until one squeezes it and pushes the squirming head outside. But woe to him who having squeezed lets go to get the necessary forceps; for the larva leaps back within, promptly dies and forms an abscess. Often I have taken as many as thirty or forty from one man. It is a melancholy comfort to find that this fly is no respecter of persons, for the Staff themselves have been known to become affected by this pest.

With the flies may be mentioned as one of the minor horrors of war in East Africa, one of the little plagues that are sent to mortify our already over-tortured flesh, the jigger flea. As if there were not already sufficient trials for us to undergo, an unkind Providence has sent this pest to rob us of what little enjoyment or elegant leisure this country might afford. True to her sex, it is the female of the species that causes all the trouble; the male is comparatively harmless. Lurking in the dust and grass of camps, she burrows beneath the skin of our toes, choosing with a calculated ferocity the tender junction of the nails with the protesting flesh. No sooner is she well ensconced therein than she commences the supreme business of life, she lays her eggs, by the million, all enclosed in a little sack. What little measure of sleep the mosquitoes, the sand flies and the stifling nights have left us, this relentless parasite destroys. For her presence is disclosed to us by itching intolerable. Then the skill of the native boys is called upon, and dusky fingers, well scrubbed in lysol, are armed with a safety pin, to pick the little interloper out intact. Curses in many languages descend upon the head of the unlucky boy who fails to remove the sack entire. For the egg-envelope once broken, abscesses and blood poisoning may result, and one's toes become an offence to surgery.

All is well, if a drop of iodine be ready to complete the well-conducted operation; but the poor soldier, whose feet, perforce, are dirty and who only has the one pair of socks, pays a heavy penalty to this little flea, that dying still has power to hurt. Dirt and the death of this tiny visitor result in painful feet that make of marching a very torture. So great a pest is this that at least five per cent. of our army, both white and native, are constantly incapacitated. Hundreds of toenails have I removed for this cause alone. Nor do the jiggers come singly, but in battalions, and often as many as fifty have to be removed from one wretched soldier's feet and legs. So we hang our socks upon our mosquito nets and take our boots to bed with us, nor do we venture to put bare feet upon the ground.

A yell in the sleeping camp at night, "Some damn thing's bit me;" and matches are struck, while a sleepy warrior hunts through his blankets for the soldier ant whose great pincers draw blood, or lurking centipede or scorpion. For in these dry, hot, dusty countries these nightly visitors come to share the warm softness of the army blanket. Next morning, sick and shivering, they come to show to me the hot red flesh or swollen limb with which the night wanderer has rewarded his involuntary host.

NIGHT IN MOROGORO

There's nothing quite so wideawake as a tropical night in Africa. At dawn the African dove commences with his long-drawn note like a boy blowing over the top of a bottle, one bird calling to another from the palms and mango trees. Then the early morning songsters wake.

There is no libel more grossly unfair than that which says the birds of Africa have no song. The yellow weaver birds sing most beautifully, as they fly from the feathery tops of the avenue of coconut palms that line the road to the clump of bamboos behind the hospital.

But they fly there no longer now, for our colonel, in a spasm of sanitation, cut down this graceful swaying clump of striped bamboos for the fear that they harboured mosquitoes. As if these few canes mattered, when our hospital was on the banks of the reed-fringed river. Morning songsters with voices of English thrushes and robins wake one to gaze upon the dawn through one's mosquito net. Small bird voices, like the chiff-chaff in May, carry on the chorus until the sun rises. Then the bird of delirium arrives and runs up the scale to a high monotonous note that would drive one mad, were it not that he and the dove, with his amphoric note, are Africa all over. A neat fawn-coloured bird this, with a long tail and dark markings on his wings.

Then as the sun rises and the early morning heat dries up the song birds' voices, the earth and the life of the palm trees drowse in the sunshine.

But at night, from late afternoon to three in the morning, when the life of trees and grasses and ponds ceases for a short while before it begins again at dawn, the air is full of the busy voices of the insect world. Until we came south to Morogoro, to the land of mangoes, coconut, palms, bamboos, we had known the shrill voice of cicadas and the harsh metallic noises of crickets in grass and trees. But here we made two new acquaintances, and charming little voices they had too. One lived in the grass and rose leaves of our garden, for the German blacksmith who lately occupied our hospital building had planted his garden with "Caroline Testout" and crimson ramblers. His voice was like the tinkling of fairy hammers upon a silver anvil. And with this fine clear note was the elusive voice of another cricket that had such a marked ventriloquial character that we could never tell whether he lived in the rose bushes or in the trees. His note was the music of silver bells upon the naked feet of rickshaw boys, the tinkle that keeps time to the soft padding of native feet in the rickshaws of Nairobi at night. At first I woke to think there were rickshaw boys dragging rubber-tyred carriages along the avenues of the town, until I found that Morogoro boasted no rickshaws and no bells for native feet.

Punctuated in all the music of fairy bands and the whirr of fairy machinery were the incessant voices of frogs. Especially if it had rained or were going to rain, the little frogs in trees and ponds sang their love songs in chorus, silenced, at times, by the deep basso of a bull frog. And often, as our heads ached and throbbed with fever at night, we felt a very lively sympathy for the French noblesse of the eighteenth century, who are said to have kept their peasants up at night beating the ponds with sticks to still the strident voices of these frogs.

With it all there is a rustling overhead in the feathery branches of the palms in the cobwebby spaces among the leaves that give the bats of Africa a home. A twitter of angry bat voices, shrill squeaks and flutters in the darkness. Then stillness--of a sudden--and the ground trembles with a far-off throbbing as a convoy of motor lorries approaching thunders past us, rumbling over the bridge and out into the darkness, driving for supplies.

The road beside the hospital was the old caravan route that ran from the Congo through Central Africa and by the Great Lakes to Bagamoyo by the sea. For centuries the Arab slaver had brought his slave caravans along this path: it may have been fever or the phantasies of disordered subconscious minds half awake in sleep, or the empty night thrilling to the music of crickets, that filled our minds with fancies in the darkness. But this road seemed alive again. For this smooth surface that now trembles to the thunder of motor lorries seemed to echo to the soft padding of millions of slave feet limping to the coast to fill the harems or to work the clove plantations of his most Oriental Majesty the Sultan of Zanzibar.

THE WATERS OF TURIANI

Halfway between the Usambara and the Central Railway, the dusty road to Morogoro crosses the Turiani River. In the woods beside the river, the tired infantry are resting at the edge of a big rock pool. Wisps of blue smoke from dying fires tell of the tea that has washed beef and biscuit down dry and dusty throats. The last company of bathers are drying in the sun upon the rocks, necks, arms and knees burnt to a sepia brown, the rest of their bodies alabaster white in the sunshine. It is three o'clock, and the drowsy heat of afternoon has hushed the bird and insect world to sleep. Only in the tree-tops is the sleepy hum of bees, still busy with the flowers, and the last twitter of soft birds' voices. Soft river laughter comes up from the rocky stream-bed below, and, softened by the distance to a poignant sweetness, the sound of church bells from Mhonda Mission floats up to us upon the west wind.

Yesterday only saw the last of Lettow's army crossing the bridge and echoed to the noise of the explosion that blew up the concrete pillars and forced our pioneers to build a wooden substitute. Alas! for the best-laid schemes of our General. The bird had escaped from the closing net, and Lettow was free to make his retreat in safety to the Southern Railway. Here at Turiani for a moment it seemed that the campaign was over. Up from the big Mission at Mhonda, the mounted troops swept out to cut off the German retreat. All unsuspected, they had made then-big flank march to meet the eastern flanking column, and cut the road behind the German force in a pincer grip. But the blind bush robbed our troopers of their sense of direction, and the long trek through waterless bush, the tsetse fly and horse-sickness that took their daily toll of all our horses reduced the speed of cavalry to little more than a walk. A mistake in a bush-covered hill in a country that was all hill and bush, and the elusive Lettow slipped out to run and hide and fight again on many another day.

SCOUTING

Of the many aspects of this campaign none perhaps is more thrilling than life on the forward patrol. For the duty of these fellows is to go forward with armed native scouts far in advance of the columns, to find out what the Germans are up to, their strength, and the disposition of their troops. Their reports they send back by native runners, who not infrequently get captured. Like wolves in the forest they live, months often elapsing without their seeing a white face, and then it is the kind of white man that they do not want to see; every man's hand against them, native as well as German, unable to light fires at night for fear of discovery, sleeping on the ground, creeping up close, for in this bush one can only get information at close quarters; always out of food, forced to smoke pungent native tobacco. They have to live on the game they shoot, and it is a hundred chances to one that the shot that gives them dinner will bring a Hun patrol to disturb the feast. Theirs is without doubt the riskiest job in such a war as this.

Here is the story of a night surprise, as it was told me. The long trek had lasted all day, to be followed by the fireless supper (how one longs for the hot tea at night!), and the deep sleep that comes to exhausted man as soon as he gets into his blankets. Drowsy sentries failed to hear the rustling in the thicket until almost too late; the alarm is given, pickets run in to wake their sleeping "bwona," all mixed up with Germans. The intelligence party scattered to all points of the compass, leaving their camp kit behind them. There was no time to do aught but pick up their rifles (that is second nature) and fly for safety to the bush. Now this actual surprise party was led by one Laudr, an Oberleutnant who had lived for years in South Africa, and had married an English wife. Laudr had the reputation of being the best shot in German East, but he missed that night, and my friend escaped, unharmed, the five shots from his revolver. Next morning, cautiously approaching the scene of last night's encounter, he found a note pinned to a tree. In it Laudr thanked him for much good food and a pair of excellent blankets, and regretted that the light had been so bad for shooting. But he left a young goat tied up to the tree and my friend's own knife and fork and plate upon the ground.

Another story this resourceful fellow told me concerning an exploit which he and a fellow I.D. man, with twenty-five of their scouts, had brought off near Arusha. They had been sent out to get information as to the strength of an enemy post in a strongly fortified stone building--the kind of half fort, half castle that the Germans build in every district as an impregnable refuge in case of native risings. With watch towers and battlements, these forts are after the style of mediaeval buildings. Equipped with food supplies and a well, they can resist any attack short of artillery. Learning from the natives that the force consisted of two German officers and about sixty Askaris, my friend determined not to send back for the column that was waiting to march from Arusha to invest the place. Between them they resolved to take the place by strategy and guile. Lying hid in the bush, they arranged with friendly natives to supply the guard with "pombe" the potent native drink. Late that night, judging from the sounds that the Kaffir beer had done its work, they crept up and disarmed the guard. Holding the outer gate they sent in word to the commandant, a Major Schneider, the administrator of the district, to surrender. He duly came from his quarters into the courtyard accompanied by his Lieutenant. "Before I consider surrender," he said, "tell me what force you've got?" "This fort is surrounded by my troops, that is enough for you," said our man. "In any case you see my men behind me, and, if you don't 'hands up,' they'll fire." And the "troops"--half-clad natives--stepped forward with levelled rifles.

The next morning the Major, still doubting, asked to see the rest of the English troops, and on being informed that these were all, would have rushed back to spring the mines that would have blown the place to pieces. But the Intelligence Officer had not wasted his time the previous night, and had very carefully cut the wires that led apparently so innocently from the central office of the fort. My friend brought this Major, a man of great importance in his district, to Dar-es-Salaam; and during the whole journey the German never ceased to complain that bluffing was a dishonourable means of warfare to employ.

On yet another occasion he had an experience that taxed his tact and strength to the utmost. In the course of his work he seized the meat-canning factory near Arusha that a certain Frau ----, in the absence of her husband, was carrying on. The enemy used to shoot wildebeest and preserve it by canning or by drying it in the sun as "biltong" for the use of the German troops. My friend was forced to burn the factory, and then it became his duty to escort this very practical lady back to our lines. This did not suit her book at all. With tears she implored him to send her to her own people. She would promise anything. Cunningly she suggested great stores of information she might impart. But he cared not for her weeping, and ordered her to pack for the long journey to Arusha. Then tears failing her she sulked, and refused to eat or leave her tent. But this found him adamant. Finally she tried the woman's wiles which should surely be irresistible to this man. But he was unmoved by all her blandishments. So surprised and indignant was he that he threatened to tell her husband of her behaviour, when he should catch him. But here it appears he made a false estimate of the value of honour and dishonour among the Huns. "A loyal German woman," she exclaimed, laughing, "is allowed to use any means to further the interests of her Fatherland. My husband will only think more highly of me when he knows." So this modern Galahad of ours turned away and ordered the lady's tent to be struck and marched her off, taking care that he himself was far removed from her presence in the caravan. "What fools you English are," she flung back at him, as he handed her into the custody that would safely hold this danger-ous apostle of *Kultur* till the end of the war.

"HUNNISHNESS"

Wearily along the road from Korogwe to Handeni toiled a little company of de-tails lately discharged from hospital and on their way forward to Division. Behind them straggled out, for half a mile or more, their line of black porters carrying blan-kets and waterproof sheets. Arms and necks and knees burnt black by many weeks of tropic sun, carrying rifle and cartridge belts and with their helmets reversed to shade their eyes from the westering sun, this little body of Rhodesians, Royal Fusiliers and South Africans covered the road in the very loose formation these details of many regiments affect. Far ahead was the advance guard of four Rhodesians and Fusiliers. Nothing further from their thoughts than war--for they were thirty miles behind Division--they were suddenly galvanised into action by the sight of the advance guard slipping into the roadside ditches and opening rapid rifle fire at some object ahead.

For at a turn of the road the advance guard perceived a large number of Askaris and several white men collected about one of our telegraph posts, while, up the post, upon the cross trees, was a white man, busily engaged with the wires. One glance was sufficient to tell these wary soldiers that the white men were wearing khaki uniforms of an unfamiliar cut and the mushroom helmet that the Hun affects. So they took cover in the ditches and opened fire, especially upon the German officer who was busily tapping our telegraph wire. Down with a great bump on the ground dropped the startled Hun, and the Askaris fled to the jungle leaving their chop boxes lying on the road. From the safe shelter of the bush the enemy reconnoitred their assailants, and taking courage from their small numbers, proceeded to envelop them by a flank movement. But the British officer in charge of the details behind, knew his job and threw out two flanking parties when he got the message from the advance guard. Our men outflanked the outflanking enemy, and soon as pretty a little engagement as one could hope to see had developed. Finding themselves partly surrounded by unsuspected strength the Germans scattered in all directions, leaving a few wounded and dead behind upon the field. There on his back, wounded in the leg and spitting fire from his revolver, was lying the German officer determined to sell his life dearly. His last shot took effect in the head of one of the Fusiliers who were charging the bush with the bayonet; up went his hands, "Kamerad, mercy!" and our officer stepped forward to disarm this chivalrous prisoner. Then they wired forward to our hospital, at that time ten miles ahead, for an ambulance, and proceeded to bury their only casualty and the dead Askaris.

Happening to be on duty, I hurried to the scene of this action in one of our ambulances, along the worst road in Africa. There I found the German officer, an Oberleutnant of the name of Zahn, lying by the roadside gazing with frightened eyes out of huge yellow spectacles. We dressed his wound and gave him an injection of morphia, a cigarette, and a good drink of brandy, and left him in the shade of a baobab tree to recover from his fears. Then I turned toward the dividing of the contents of captured chop boxes that was being carried out under the direction of the officer in charge. On occasions such as these, the men were rewarded with the only really square meal they had often had for days; for the Hun is a past master in the art of doing himself well, and his chopboxes are always full of new bread, chocolate, sardines and many little delicacies. I stepped forward to claim the two Red Cross boxes that had obviously been the property of the German doctor, and with some difficulty--for no soldier likes to be robbed of his spoil--I managed to establish the right of the hospital to them. In the boxes were not only a fine selection of drugs and surgical dressings and a bottle of brandy, but also the doctor's ammunition. And such ammunition too. Huge black-powder cartridges with large leaden bullets; they would only fit an elephant gun; and yet this was the kind of weapon this doctor found necessary to bring to protect himself against British soldiers. Had that doctor been caught with his rifle he would have deserved to be shot on the spot. Nor were our men in the best of moods; for they had seen the dead Fusilier, and were furious at the wounds these huge lead slugs create.

The orderlies then lifted the German officer tenderly into the ambulance; and the prisoner, now feeling full of the courage that morphia and brandy give, beckoned to me. "Meine Uhr in meiner Tasche," he said, pointing to his torn trouser. "Well, what about it?" I asked. Again he mentioned his watch in his pocket, and looked at his torn trouser. "Do you suggest," I said sternly, "that a British soldier has taken your beastly watch." "No, no, not for worlds," he exclaimed; "I merely wish to mention the fact that when I went into action I had had a large gold watch and a large gold chain, and much gold coin in my pocket. And now," he said, "behold! I have no watch or chain." "What," I said again, "do you suggest that these soldiers are thieves?" "No! Not at all; but when I was wounded the soldiers, running up in their anxiety to help me and dress my wound" (as a matter of fact they had run up to bayonet him, had not the officer intervened, for this swine had forfeited his right to mercy by emptying his revolver first and then surrendering) "inadvertently cut away my pocket in slitting up my trouser leg." "Then your watch," I continued coldly, "is still lying on the field, or, if a soldier should discover it, he will deliver it to General Headquarters, from whence it will be sent to you." Sure enough that evening the sergeant-major in charge of the rearguard came in with the missing watch and chain.

Later, we learned, from diaries captured on German prisoners, what manner of brute this Zahn was.

FROM MINDEN TO MOROGODO

Judge of my surprise when, one morning in hospital at Morogoro, a fellow walked in to see me whose face reminded me of times, two years back, when I was in the Prisoners of War Camp at Minden in Westphalia. He showed a fatter and more wholesome face certainly, he was clean and well dressed, but still, unmistakably it was the man to whom I used to take an occasional book or chocolate when he lay behind the wire of the inner prison there. "It can't be you?" I said illogically. But it was.

But what a change these two years had wrought! Now an officer in the Royal Flying Corps, the ribbon of the Military Cross bearing witness to many a risky reconnaissance over the Rufigi Valley; but then a dirty mechanic in the French Aviation Corps and a prisoner. But in December, 1914, there were no fat or clean English soldiers in German prisons.

And, as I looked, my mind went back to a wet morning when, the German sentry's back being turned, a French soldier, working on the camp road, dug his way near to the door of my hut and, still digging, told me that there was an Englishman in the French camp, who wanted particularly to see me. So that afternoon I walked boldly into the French camp as if I had important business there, and found my way to the further hut. There lying on a straw mattress, incredibly lousy and sandwiched between a Turco from Morocco and a Senegalese negro soldier, I found a white man, who jumped up to see me and was extraordinarily glad to find that his message had borne fruit. Clad in the tattered but still unmistakable uniform of a French artilleryman, three months' beard upon his face, with white wax-like cheeks, blue nose and a dreadfully hunted expression, stood this six emaciated feet of England. Drawing me aside to a sheltered corner he told me his story; how, despairing of a job in our Flying Corps at the commencement of the war, he had joined the French Aviation Corps as a mechanic, and how he had been taken prisoner early in September, 1914, when the engine of his aeroplane failed and he descended to earth in the middle of a marching column of the enemy. Of the early months of captivity from September to December in Minden he told me many things. He and all the others lived in an open field exposed to all the Westphalian winter weather, with no blankets, nothing but what he now wore. They lived in holes in a wet clay field like rats and--like rats they fought for the offal and pigwash on which the German jailors fed them twice a day. Now he had been moved into a long hut, open on the inner side that looked to the enclosed central square of the lager, but well enclosed outside by a triple barbed wire fence.

"Why do they put you in with coloured men?" I asked, as I looked at his bedfellows.

"Oh, that's because I'm an Englishman, you know," he said. "When I came here the commandant, finding who I was, was pleased to be facetious. 'Brothers in arms, glorious,' he chuckled, as he ordered my particular abode here. 'You, of course, don't object to sleep with a comrade,' he said, with heavy German humour. And I wanted to tell him, had I only dared, that I'd rather sleep with a nigger from Senegal than with him."

"How about the lice?" I said, for it was not possible to avoid seeing them on the thin piece of flannelette that was his blanket.

"Oh, I'm used to them now. Time was when I hunted my clothes all day long, but now--nothing matters; in fact, I rather think they keep me warm."

So I was quick and glad to help in the little way I could. Not that there was much that I could do. But I at least had one good meal a day and two of German prison food, but he had only three bowls of prisoner's stew and soup. Lest you might think that I exaggerate, I will tell you exactly what he had, and you may judge what manner of diet it was for a big Englishman. Five ounces of black bread a day, part of barley and part of potato, the rest of rye and wheat; for breakfast, a pint of lukewarm artificial coffee made of acorns burnt with maize, no sugar; sauerkraut and cabbage in hot water twice a day, occasionally some boiled barley or rice or oatmeal, and now and then--almost by a miracle, so rare were the occasions--a small bit of horseflesh in the soup. Could one wonder at the wolfish look upon his face, the dreary hopelessness of his expression? And on this diet he had fatigues to do; but on those days of hard toil there was also a little extra bread and an inch of

German sausage.

But I could get some things from the canteen by bribing the German orderly who brought our midday food, and I had some books. So the sun shone, for a time, on Minden.

Nor was this fellow alone in these unhappy surroundings. There with him were English civilian prisoners, clerks and school-teachers, technical and engineering instructors, who once taught in German schools and worked at Essen or in the shipyards. These wretched civilians, until they were removed to Ruhleben, were not in much better case; but they might, at least, sleep together on indescribable straw palliasses. Then they were together; there was comfort in that at least.

By a strange turn of Fortune's wheel this very camp was placed upon the site of the battlefield of Minden, when, as our guards would tell us, an undegenerate England fought with the great Frederick against the French.

Moved to another camp this fellow had escaped by crawling under the barbed wire on a dirty wet night in winter when the sentry had turned his well-clothed back against the northern gale.

A MORAL DISASTER

All the Army is looking for the gunnery lieutenant, H.M.S. ----. Time indeed may soften the remembrance of the evil he has done us, and in the dim future, when we get to Dar-es-Salaam, we may even relent sufficiently to drink with him; but now, just halfway along the dusty road from Handeni to Morogoro, we feel that there's no torture yet devised that would be a fitting punishment.

Strange how frail a thing is human happiness, that the small matter of a mis-directed 12-inch shell should blight the lives of a whole army and tinge our thirsty souls with melancholy. For this clumsy projectile that left the muzzle of the gun with the intention of wrecking the railway station in Dar-es-Salaam became, by evil chance, deflected in its path and struck the brewery instead. Not the office or the non-essential part of the building, but the very heart, the mainspring of the whole, the precious vats and machinery for making beer. And there will be no more "lager" in German East Africa until the war is over.

All the long hot march from Kilimanjaro down the Pangani River and along the dusty, thirsty plains we had all been sustained by the thought that one day we would strike the Central Railway and, finding some sufficient pretext to snatch some leave, would swiftly board a train for Dar-es-Salaam and drink from the Fountain of East Africa. The one bright hope that upheld us, the one beautiful dream that dragged weary footsteps southward over that waterless, thorny desert was the occupation of the brewery. We had heard its fame all over the country, we had met a few of its precious bottles full at the Coast, had found some empty--in the many German plantations we had searched.

Now "Ichabod" is written large upon our resting-places, the joy of life departed, the sparkle gone from bright eyes that longed for victory, and, as King's Regulations have it, alarm and consternation have spread through all ranks. Even the accompanying news of the tears of the Hun population in Dar-es-Salaam at this wanton destruction, failed to comfort us.

The Navy were very nice about it. They were just as sorry as we, they said. The gunner had been put under observation as a criminal lunatic, we understood. But they had just come from Zanzibar, and every one knows that all good things are to be found in that isle of clover. All the excuses in the world won't give us back our promised beer again.

THE ANGEL OF MOROGORO

Standing on the river bridge that crossed the main road into Morogoro was a slender figure in the white uniform of a nursing sister. In one hand a tiny Union Jack, in the other a white flag.

"Don't shoot," she cried, "I'm an Englishwoman;" and the bearded South African troopers, who were reconnoitring the approaches to their town, stopped and smiled down upon her. "Take this letter to General Smuts, please; it is from the German General von Lettow;" and handing it to one of them, she shook hands with the other and told him how she had been waiting for two years for him to come and release her from her prison. For this nursing sister had been behind prison bars for two years in German East Africa, and you may imagine how she had longed for the day when the English would come and set her free.

This was Sister Mabel, the only nursing sister we had in Morogoro for the first four months of our occupation. Her memory lives in the hearts of hundreds of our wretched soldiers, who were brought with malaria or dysentery to the shelter of our hospital. In spite of the fact that she was one of the trained English nursing sisters of the English Universities Mission in German East Africa, she was imprisoned with the rest of the Allied civil population of that German colony from the commencement of war until the time that Smuts had come to break the prison bars and let the wretched captives free. She had had her share of insult, indignity, shame and ill-treatment at the hands of her savage gaolers. But in that slender body lived a very gallant soul, and that gave her spirit to dare and courage to endure. So when we occupied Morogoro and Lettow fled with his troops to the mountains, this very splendid sister gave up her chance of leave well-earned to come to nurse for us in our hospital. The Germans had failed to break the spirits of these civilian prisoners, and they had full knowledge of the army that was slowly moving south from Kilimanjaro to redress the balance of unsuccessful military enterprise in the past. One can imagine the state of mind of these wretched people when the news of our ill-fated attack on Tanga in 1914 arrived; when they heard of our Indian troops being made prisoners at Jassin, and saw from the cock-a-hoop attitude of the Hun that all was well for German arms in East Africa. Then when Nemesis was approaching, the German commandant came to their prison to make amends for past wrongs. "I am desolated to think," he unctuously explained, "that you ladies have had so little comfort in this camp in the past, and I have come to make things easier for you now. The English Government," he continued with an ingratiating smile, "have now begun to treat our prisoners in England better, and I hasten to return good to you for the evils that our women have suffered at the hands of your Government. Is there anything I can do for you? Would you like native servants? Would you care to go for walks?" But these brave women answered that they had done without servants and walks for two years now, and they could endure a little longer. "What do you mean," he exclaimed in anger, "by 'a little longer?'" But they answered nothing, and he knew the news of our advance had come to them within their prison cage. "Would you care to nurse our wounded soldiers?" he said more softly. Sister Mabel said she would. So now for the first time she is given a native servant, carried in state down the mountain-side in a hammock, and installed in the German hospital in Morogoro. There, in virtue of the excellence of her work and knowledge, she was given charge of badly wounded German officers, and received with acid smiles of welcome from the German sisters.

To her, at the evacuation of the town, had Lettow come, and, giving her a letter to General Smuts, had asked her to put in a good word for the German woman and children he was leaving behind him to our tender mercies. "There is no need of letters to ask for protection for German women," she told him; "you know how well they've been treated in Wilhemstal and Mombo." But he insisted, and she consented, and so the bearded troopers found this English emissary of Lettow's waiting for them upon the river bridge.

Back came General Smuts's answer, "Tell the women of Morogoro that, if they stay in their houses, they have nothing to fear from British troops, nor will one house be entered, if only they stay indoors." And the Army was as good as the word of their Chief; for no occupied house, not one German chicken, not a cabbage was taken from any German house or garden.

And now the despised and rejected English Sister had become the "Oberschwester," and her German fellow nursing sisters had to take their orders from her. But she exercised a difficult authority very kindly and adopted a very cool and distant attitude toward them. But there was one thing she never did again: she never spoke German any more, but gave all her orders and held all dealings with the enemy in Swahili, the native language, or in English. In this she was adamant.

Now, indeed, had the great work of her life begun; for into those four months she crammed the devotion of a lifetime. Always full to overcrowding, never less than 600 patients where we had only the equipment for 200, the whole hospital looked to her for the nursing that is so essential in modern medicine and surgery. For nurses are now an absolute necessity for medical and surgical work of modern times, and we could get no other sisters. The railway was broken, the bridges down, and where could we look for help or hospital comforts or medical necessities? We had pushed on faster than our supplies, and with the equipment of a Casualty Clearing Station we had to do the work of a Stationary Hospital. No beds save those we took over from the German Hospital, no sheets nor linen. Can one wonder that she was everywhere and anywhere at all homes and in all places? Six o'clock in the morning found her in the wards; she alone of all of us could find no time to rest in the afternoon; a step upon the verandah where she slept beside the bad pneumonias and black-water fever cases found her always up and ready to help. Nor was her job finished in the nursing; she was our housekeeper too. For she alone could run the German woman cook, could speak Swahili, and keep order among the native boys, buy eggs and fruit and chickens from the natives, so that our sick might not want for the essentially fresh foods. Then at last the railway opened up a big Stationary Hospital, our Casualty Clearing Station moved further to the bush, and Sister Mabel's work was done. But there was no elegant leisure for her when she arrived at the Coast to take the leave she long had earned in England. An Australian transport had some cases of cerebro-spinal meningitis aboard, and wanted Sisters, and, as if she had not already had enough to do, took her with them through the sunny South Atlantic seas to the home that had not seen her since she left for Tropical Africa five weary years before.

THE WILL TO DESTROY

The journey from Morogoro to Dar-es-Salaam is a most interesting experience, a perfect object lesson in the kind of futile railway destruction that defeats its own ends. For Lettow and his advisers said that our long wait at M'syeh had ruined our chances. Complete destruction of the railway and of all the rolling stock would hold us up for the valuable two months until the rains were due. Our means of supply all that time would be, perforce, the long road haul by motor lorry, by mule or ox or donkey transport, two hundred miles, from the Northern Railway. Lettow bet on the rains and the completeness of the railway destruction he would cause; but he bargained without his visitors. Little did he know the resource and capacity of our Indian sappers and miners, our Engineer and Pioneer battalions.

They threw themselves on broken culverts and wrecked bridges; with only hand tools, so short of equipment were they, they drove piles and built up girders on heaps of sleepers and made the bridges safe again. Saving every scrap of chain, every abandoned German tool, making shift here, extemporising there, bending steel rails on hand forges, utilising the scrap heaps the enemy had left, they finally won and brought the first truck through, in triumph, in six weeks. But the first carriage was no Pullman car. It exemplified the resource of our men and illustrated the idea that proved Lettow wrong. For we adapted the engines of Ford and Bico motor cars and motor lorries to the bogie wheels of German trucks and sent a little fleet of motor cars along the railway. Light and very speedy, these little trains sped along, each dragging its thirty tons of food and supplies for the army then 120 miles from Dar-es-Salaam.

This adaptation of the internal combustion engine to fixed rails may not be new, but it was unexpected by Lettow. And the German engineers left it a little too late; they panicked at the last and destroyed wholesale, but without intelligence. True, they put an explosive charge into the cylinders of all their big engines and left us to get new cylinders cast in Scotland. They blew out the grease boxes of the trucks; but their performance, on the whole, was amateurish. For they blew up, with dynamite, the masonry of many bridges and contented themselves that the girders lay in the river below. But this was child's play to our Sappers and Miners. With hand jacks they lifted the girders and piled up sleepers, one by one beneath, until the girder was lifted to rail level again. Now any engineer can tell you that the only way to destroy a bridge is to cut the girder. This would send us humming over the cables to Glasgow to get it replaced. It was what they did do on the most important bridge over Ruwu River, but in their anxiety to do the thing properly there--and they reckoned four months' hard work would find us with a new bridge still unfinished--they forgot the old deviation, an old spur that ran round the big span that crossed the river and lay buried in the jungle growth. In ten days we had opened up this old deviation, laid new rails, and had the line re-opened. When I passed down the line we took the long way round by this long-abandoned track and left the useless bridge upon our right. Much method but little intelligence was shown in the destruction of the railway lines; for they often failed to remove the points, contenting themselves with removing the rails and hiding them in the jungle.

The German engineers must have wept at the orgy of devastation that followed: blind fury alone seemed to animate this scene of blind destruction. At N'geri N'geri and Ruwu they first broke the middle one of the three big spans and ran the rolling stock, engines, sleeping cars, a beautiful ambulance train, trucks and carriages, pell mell into the river-bed below. But the wreckage piled up in a heap 60 feet high and soon was level with the bridge again. So they broke the other spans and ran most of the rest of the rolling stock through the gaps. When these, too, had piled up, they finally ran the remainder of the rolling stock down the embankments and into the jungle. Then they set fire to the three huge heaps of wreckage, and the glare lit the heavens for nearly a hundred miles. But the almost uninjured railway trucks that had run their little race, down embankments into the bush, were saved to run again.

Into Morogoro station steamed the trains with the German lettering and freight and tare directions, carefully undisturbed, printed on their sides. To us it seemed that the destruction of an ambulance train that had in the past relied upon the Red Cross and our forbearance, was cutting it rather fine and putting a new interpretation upon the Geneva Convention. The Germans, however, argue that the English are such swine they would have used it to carry supplies as well as sick and wounded.

And what a magnificent railway it was, and what splendid rolling stock they had! Steel sleepers, big heavy rails, low gradients, excellent cuts and bridge work; cuttings through rock smoothed as if by sandpaper and crevices filled with concrete. Fine concrete gutters along the curves, such ballasting as one sees on the North-Western Railway. Nothing cheap or flimsy about the culverts. Railway stations built regardless of cost and the possibility of traffic; stone houses and waiting-rooms roofed with soft red tiles that are in such contrast to the red-washed corrugated iron roofing one sees in British East Africa. Expensive weighbridges where it seemed there was nothing but a few natives with an occasional load of mangoes and bananas. Here was an indifference to mere dividends; at every point evidence abounded of a lavish display of public money through a generous Colonial Office. For in the Wilhelmstrasse this colony was ever the apple of their eye, and money was always ready for East African enterprises.

Yet the planters complain, just as planters do all over the world, of the indifference of Governments and the parsimony of executive officials. A Greek rubber planter told me, from the standpoint of an intelligent and benevolent neutrality (and who so likely to know the meaning of benevolence in neutral obligations as a Greek?), that the Government charged huge freights on this line, killed young enterprise by excessive charges, gave no rebates even to German planters, and in other ways seemed indifferent to the fortunes of the sisal and rubber planters. True they built the railway; but what use to a planter to build a line and rob him of his profits in the freight? This gentleman of ancient Sparta frankly liked the Germans and found them just; and he was in complete agreement with the native policy that made every black brother do his job of work, the whole year round, at a rate of pay that fully satisfied this Greek employer's views on the minimum wage.

DAR-ES-SALAAM
(The Haven of Peace)

This town is indeed a Haven of Peace for our weary soldiers. The only rest in a really civilised place that they have had after many hundreds of miles of road and forest and trackless thirsty bush. In the cool wards of the big South African Hospital many of them enjoy the only rest that they have known for months. Fever-stricken wrecks are they of the men that marched so eagerly to Kilimanjaro nine weary months before. Months of heat and thirst and tiredness, of malaria that left them burning under trees by the roadside till the questing ambulance could find them, of dysentery that robbed their nights of sleep, of dust and flies and savage bush fighting. And now they lie between cool sheets and watch the sisters as they flit among the shadows of cool, shaded wards. Only a short three months before and this was the "Kaiserhof," the first hotel on the East Coast of Africa, as the German manager, with loud boastfulness, proclaimed.

There had been a time when we doctors, then at Nairobi and living in comfortable mosquito-proof houses, had blamed the men for drinking unboiled water and for discarding their mosquito nets. But even doctors sometimes live and learn, and those of us who went right forward with the troops came to know how impracticable it was to carry out the Army Order that bade a man drink only boiled water and sleep beneath a net. Late in the night the infantryman staggers to the camp that lies among thorn bushes, hungry and tired and full of fever. How then could one expect him to put up a mosquito net in the pitch-black darkness in a country where every tree has got a thorn? Long ago the army's mosquito nets have adorned the prickly bushes of the waterless deserts. "Tuck your mosquito net well in at night," so runs the Army Order. But what does it profit him to tuck in the net when dysentery drags him from his blanket every hour at night?

From the verandah of the hospital the soldier sees the hospital ship all lighted up at night with red and green lights, the ship that's going to take him out of this infernal climate to where the mosquitoes are uninfected and tsetse flies bite no more. And there are no regrets that the rainy season is commencing, and this is no longer a campaign for the white soldier. On the sunlit slopes of Wynberg he will contemplate the white sands of Muizenberg and recover the strength that he will want again, in four months' time, in the swamps of the Rufigi. Now the time has come for the black troops to see through the rest of the rainy season, to sit upon the highlands and watch, across miles of intervening swamp, the tiny points of fire that are the camp fires of German Askaris.

Through the shady streets of this lovely town wander our soldier invalids in their blue and grey hospital uniforms, along the well-paved roads, neat boulevards, immaculate gardens and avenues of mangoes and feathery palm trees. Along the sea front at night in front of the big German hospital that now houses our surgical cases, you will find these invalids walking past the cemetery where the "good Huns" sleep, sitting on the beach, enjoying the cool sea breeze that sweeps into the town on the North-East Monsoon.

Imagine the loveliest little land-locked harbour in the world, a white strip of coral and of sand, groves of feathery palms, graceful shady mangoes, huge baobab trees that were here when Vasco da Gama's soldiers trod these native paths; and among them fine stone houses, soft red-tiled roofs, verandahs all screened with mosquito gauze and excellently well laid out, and you have Dar-es-Salaam.

Nothing is left of the old Arab village that was here for centuries before the German planted this garden-city. Sloping coral sands, where Arab dhows have beached themselves for ages past, are now supporting the newest and most modern of tropical warehouses and wharves, electric cranes, travelling cargo-carriers and a well-planned railway goods yard that takes the freights of Hamburg to the heart of Central Africa.

It must be pain and grief to the German men and women whom our clemency allows to occupy their houses, throng the streets and read the daily Reuter cablegram, to see this town, the apple of their eye, defiled by the "dirty English" the hated "beefs," as they call us from a mistaken idea of our fondness for that tinned delicacy.

But the soldiers' daily swim in the harbour is undisturbed by sharks, and the feel of the soft water is like satin to their bodies. Not for these spare and slender figures the prickly heat that torments fat and beery German bodies and makes sea-bathing anathema to the Hun. On German yachts the lucky few of officers and men are carried on soft breezes round the harbour and outside the harbour mouth in the evening coolness.

Arab dhows sail lazily over the blue sea from Zanzibar. If one could dream, one could picture the corsairs' red flag and the picturesque Arab figure standing high in the stern beside the tiller, and fancy would portray the freight of spices and cloves that they should bring from the plantations of Pemba and Zanzibar. But there are no dusky beauties now aboard these ships; and their freight is rations and other hum-drum prosaic things for our troops. The red pirate's flag has become the red ensign of our merchant marine.

All the caravan routes from Central Africa debouch upon this place and Baga-moyo. Bismarck looks out from the big avenue that bears his name across the har-bour to where the D.O.A.L. ship *Tabora* lies on her side; further on he looks at the sunken dry dock and a stranded German Imperial Yacht. It would seem as if a little "blood and iron" had come home to roost; even as the sea birds do upon his forehead. The grim mouth, that once told Thiers that he would leave the women of France nothing but their eyes to weep with, is mud-splashed by our passing motor lorries.

The more I see of this place the more I like it. Everything to admire but the water supply, the sanitation, the Huns and Hunnesses and a few other beastlinesses. One can admire even the statue of Wissmann, the great explorer, that looks with fixed eyes to the Congo in the eye of the setting sun. He is symbolical of everything that a boastful Germany can pretend to. For at his feet is a native Askari looking upward, with adoring eye, to the "Bwona Kuba" who has given him the priceless boon of militarism, while with both hands the soldier lays a flag--the imperial flag of Germany--across a prostrate lion at his feet. "Putting it acrost the British lion," as I heard one of our soldiers remark.

"*Si monumentum requiris circumspice*" as the Latins say; or, as Tommy would translate, "If you want to see a bit of orl-right, look at what the Navy has done to this 'ere blinking town." The Governor's palace, where is it? The bats now roost in the roofless timbers that the 12-inch shells have left. What of the three big German liners that fled to this harbour for protection and painted their upper works green to harmonise with the tops of the palm trees and thus to escape observation of our cruisers? Ask the statue of Bismarck. He'll know, for he has been looking at them for a year now. The *Tabora* lies on her side half submerged in water; the *Koenig* lies beached at the harbour mouth in a vain attempt to block the narrow entrance and keep us out; the *Feldmarschal* now on her way upon the high seas, to carry valuable food for us and maybe to be torpedoed by her late owners. The crowning insult, that this ship should have recently been towed by the *ex-Professor Woermann*--another captured prize.

What of the two dry docks that were to make Dar-es-Salaam the only ship-repairing station on the East Coast? One lies sunk at the harbour mouth, shortly, however, to be raised and utilised by us; the other in the harbour, sunk too soon, an ineffectual sacrifice.

Germans and their womenfolk crowd the streets; many of the former quite young and obvious deserters, the latter, thick of body and thicker of ankle, walk the town unmolested. Not one insult or injury has ever been offered to a German woman in this whole campaign. But these "victims of our bow and spear" are not a bit pleased. The calm indifference that our men display towards them leaves them hurt and chagrined. Better far to receive any kind of attention than to be ignored by these indifferent soldiers. What a tribute to their charms that the latest Hun fashion, latest in Dar-es-Salaam, but latest by three years in Paris or London, should provoke no glance of interest on Sunday mornings! One feels that they long to pose as martyrs, and that our quixotic chivalry cuts them to the quick.

There have been many bombardments of the forts of this town, and huge dug-outs for the whole population have been constructed. Great underground towns, twenty feet below the surface, all roofed in with steel railway sleepers. No wonder that many of the inhabitants fled to Morogoro and Tabora. What a wicked thing of the Englander to shell an "undefended" town! The search-lights and the huge gun positions and the maze of trenches, barbed wire and machine-gun emplacements hewn out of the living rock, of course, to the Teuton mind, do not constitute defence.

But you must not think that we have had it all our own way in this sea-warfare here. For in Zanzibar harbour the masts of H.M.S. *Pegasus* peep above the water--a mute reminder of the 20th September, 1914. For on that fatal day, attested to by sixteen graves in the cemetery, and more on an island near, a traitor betrayed the fact that our ship was anchored and under repairs in harbour and the rest of the fleet away. Up sailed the *Koenigsberg* and opened fire; and soon our poor ship was adrift and half destroyed. A gallant attempt to beach her was foiled by the worst bit of bad luck--she slipped off the edge of the bank into deep water. But even this incident was not without its splendid side; for the little patrol tug originally captured from the enemy, threw itself into the line of fire in a vain attempt to gain time for the *Pegasus* to clear. But the cruiser's sharp stern cut her to the water-line and sank her; and as her commander swam away, the *Koenigsberg* passed, hailed and threw a lifebuoy. "Can we give you a hand?" said the very chivalrous commander of this German ship. "No; go to Hamburg," said our hero, as he swam to shore to save himself to fight again, on many a day, upon another ship.

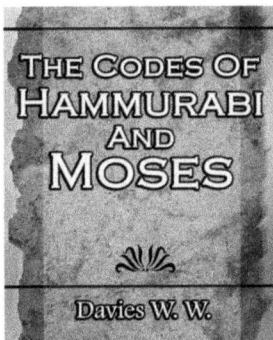

The Codes Of Hammurabi And Moses
W. W. Davies

The discovery of the Hammurabi Code is one of the greatest achievements of archaeology, and is of paramount interest, not only to the student of the Bible, but also to all those interested in ancient history...

Religion   **ISBN:** *1-59462-338-4*

Pages:132

MSRP $12.95

QTY

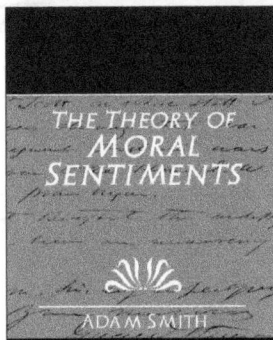

The Theory of Moral Sentiments
Adam Smith

This work from 1749. contains original theories of conscience amd moral judgment and it is the foundation for systemof morals.

Philosophy   **ISBN:** *1-59462-777-0*

Pages:536

MSRP $19.95

QTY

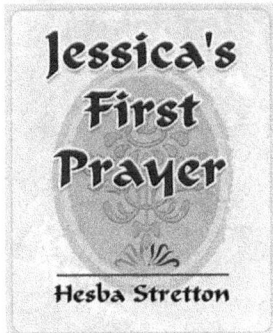

Jessica's First Prayer
Hesba Stretton

In a screened and secluded corner of one of the many railway-bridges which span the streets of London there could be seen a few years ago, from five o'clock every morning until half past eight, a tidily set-out coffee-stall, consisting of a trestle and board, upon which stood two large tin cans, with a small fire of charcoal burning under each so as to keep the coffee boiling during the early hours of the morning when the work-people were thronging into the city on their way to their daily toil...

Pages:84

Childrens   **ISBN:** *1-59462-373-2*

MSRP $9.95

QTY

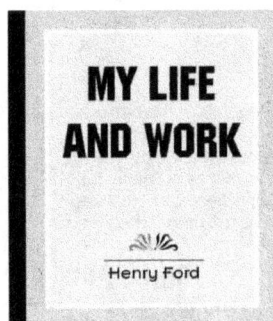

My Life and Work
Henry Ford

Henry Ford revolutionized the world with his implementation of mass production for the Model T automobile. Gain valuable business insight into his life and work with his own auto-biography... "We have only started on our development of our country we have not as yet, with all our talk of wonderful progress, done more than scratch the surface. The progress has been wonderful enough but..."

Pages:300

Biographies/   **ISBN:** *1-59462-198-5*

MSRP $21.95

QTY

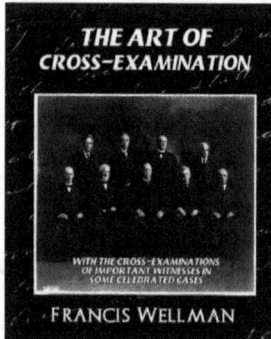

The Art of Cross-Examination
Francis Wellman

QTY

I presume it is the experience of every author, after his first book is published upon an important subject, to be almost overwhelmed with a wealth of ideas and illustrations which could readily have been included in his book, and which to his own mind, at least, seem to make a second edition inevitable. Such certainly was the case with me; and when the first edition had reached its sixth impression in five months, I rejoiced to learn that it seemed to my publishers that the book had met with a sufficiently favorable reception to justify a second and considerably enlarged edition. ..

Reference   ISBN: *1-59462-647-2*

Pages:412

MSRP $19.95

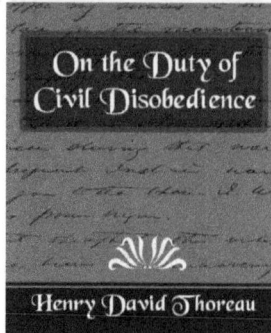

On the Duty of Civil Disobedience
Henry David Thoreau

QTY

Thoreau wrote his famous essay, On the Duty of Civil Disobedience, as a protest against an unjust but popular war and the immoral but popular institution of slave-owning. He did more than write—he declined to pay his taxes, and was hauled off to gaol in consequence. Who can say how much this refusal of his hastened the end of the war and of slavery ?

Law   ISBN: *1-59462-747-9*

Pages:48

MSRP $7.45

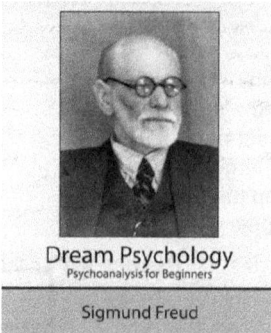

Dream Psychology Psychoanalysis for Beginners
Sigmund Freud

QTY

Sigmund Freud, born Sigismund Schlomo Freud (May 6, 1856 - September 23, 1939), was a Jewish-Austrian neurologist and psychiatrist who co-founded the psychoanalytic school of psychology. Freud is best known for his theories of the unconscious mind, especially involving the mechanism of repression; his redefinition of sexual desire as mobile and directed towards a wide variety of objects; and his therapeutic techniques, especially his understanding of transference in the therapeutic relationship and the presumed value of dreams as sources of insight into unconscious desires.

Psychology   ISBN: *1-59462-905-6*

Pages:196

MSRP $15.45

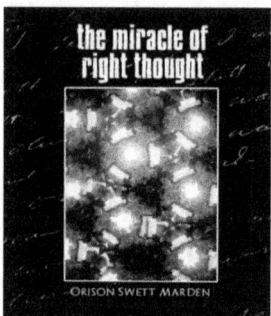

The Miracle of Right Thought
Orison Swett Marden

QTY

Believe with all of your heart that you will do what you were made to do. When the mind has once formed the habit of holding cheerful, happy, prosperous pictures, it will not be easy to form the opposite habit. It does not matter how improbable or how far away this realization may see, or how dark the prospects may be, if we visualize them as best we can, as vividly as possible, hold tenaciously to them and vigorously struggle to attain them, they will gradually become actualized, realized in the life. But a desire, a longing without endeavor, a yearning abandoned or held indifferently will vanish without realization.

Self Help   ISBN: *1-59462-644-8*

Pages:360

MSRP $25.45

The Rosicrucian Cosmo-Conception Mystic Christianity *by Max Heindel* ISBN: *1-59462-188-8* **$38.95**
The Rosicrucian Cosmo-conception is not dogmatic, neither does it appeal to any other authority than the reason of the student. It is: not controversial, but is: sent forth in the, hope that it may help to clear... New Age/Religion Pages 646

Abandonment To Divine Providence *by Jean-Pierre de Caussade* ISBN: *1-59462-228-0* **$25.95**
"The Rev. Jean Pierre de Caussade was one of the most remarkable spiritual writers of the Society of Jesus in France in the 18th Century. His death took place at Toulouse in 1751. His works have gone through many editions and have been republished... Inspirational/Religion Pages 400

Mental Chemistry *by Charles Haanel* ISBN: *1-59462-192-6* **$23.95**
Mental Chemistry allows the change of material conditions by combining and appropriately utilizing the power of the mind. Much like applied chemistry creates something new and unique out of careful combinations of chemicals the mastery of mental chemistry... New Age Pages 354

The Letters of Robert Browning and Elizabeth Barret Barrett 1845-1846 vol II ISBN: *1-59462-193-4* **$35.95**
by Robert Browning and Elizabeth Barrett Biographies Pages 596

Gleanings In Genesis (volume I) *by Arthur W. Pink* ISBN: *1-59462-130-6* **$27.45**
Appropriately has Genesis been termed "the seed plot of the Bible" for in it we have, in germ form, almost all of the great doctrines which are afterwards fully developed in the books of Scripture which follow... Religion/Inspirational Pages 420

The Master Key *by L. W. de Laurence* ISBN: *1-59462-001-6* **$30.95**
In no branch of human knowledge has there been a more lively increase of the spirit of research during the past few years than in the study of Psychology, Concentration and Mental Discipline. The requests for authentic lessons in Thought Control, Mental Discipline and... New Age/Business Pages 422

The Lesser Key Of Solomon Goetia *by L. W. de Laurence* ISBN: *1-59462-092-X* **$9.95**
This translation of the first book of the "Lerngton" which is now for the first time made accessible to students of Talismanic Magic was done, after careful collation and edition, from numerous Ancient Manuscripts in Hebrew, Latin, and French... New Age/Occult Pages 92

Rubaiyat Of Omar Khayyam *by Edward Fitzgerald* ISBN:*1-59462-332-5* **$13.95**
Edward Fitzgerald, whom the world has already learned, in spite of his own efforts to remain within the shadow of anonymity, to look upon as one of the rarest poets of the century, was born at Bredfield, in Suffolk, on the 31st of March, 1809. He was the third son of John Purcell... Music Pages 172

Ancient Law *by Henry Maine* ISBN: *1-59462-128-4* **$29.95**
The chief object of the following pages is to indicate some of the earliest ideas of mankind, as they are reflected in Ancient Law, and to point out the relation of those ideas to modern thought. Religiom/History Pages 452

Far-Away Stories *by William J. Locke* ISBN: *1-59462-129-2* **$19.45**
"Good wine needs no bush, but a collection of mixed vintages does. And this book is just such a collection. Some of the stories I do not want to remain buried for ever in the museum files of dead magazine-numbers an author's not unpardonable vanity..." Fiction Pages 272

Life of David Crockett *by David Crockett* ISBN: *1-59462-250-7* **$27.45**
"Colonel David Crockett was one of the most remarkable men of the times in which he lived. Born in humble life, but gifted with a strong will, an indomitable courage, and unremitting perseverance... Biographies/New Age Pages 424

Lip-Reading *by Edward Nitchie* ISBN: *1-59462-206-X* **$25.95**
Edward B. Nitchie, founder of the New York School for the Hard of Hearing, now the Nitchie School of Lip-Reading, Inc, wrote "LIP-READING Principles and Practice". The development and perfecting of this meritorious work on lip-reading was an undertaking... How-to Pages 400

A Handbook of Suggestive Therapeutics, Applied Hypnotism, Psychic Science ISBN: *1-59462-214-0* **$24.95**
by Henry Munro Health/New Age/Health/Self-help Pages 376

A Doll's House: and Two Other Plays *by Henrik Ibsen* ISBN: *1-59462-112-8* **$19.95**
Henrik Ibsen created this classic when in revolutionary 1848 Rome. Introducing some striking concepts in playwriting for the realist genre, this play has been studied the world over. Fiction/Classics/Plays 308

The Light of Asia *by sir Edwin Arnold* ISBN: *1-59462-204-3* **$13.95**
In this poetic masterpiece, Edwin Arnold describes the life and teachings of Buddha. The man who was to become known as Buddha to the world was born as Prince Gautama of India but he rejected the worldly riches and abandoned the reigns of power when... Religion/History/Biographies Pages 170

The Complete Works of Guy de Maupassant *by Guy de Maupassant* ISBN: *1-59462-157-8* **$16.95**
"For days and days, nights and nights, I had dreamed of that first kiss which was to consecrate our engagement, and I knew not on what spot I should put my lips..." Fiction/Classics Pages 240

The Art of Cross-Examination *by Francis L. Wellman* ISBN: *1-59462-309-0* **$26.95**
Written by a renowned trial lawyer, Wellman imparts his experience and uses case studies to explain how to use psychology to extract desired information through questioning. How-to/Science/Reference Pages 408

Answered or Unanswered? *by Louisa Vaughan* ISBN: *1-59462-248-5* **$10.95**
Miracles of Faith in China Religion Pages 112

The Edinburgh Lectures on Mental Science (1909) *by Thomas* ISBN: *1-59462-008-3* **$11.95**
This book contains the substance of a course of lectures recently given by the writer in the Queen Street Hall, Edinburgh. Its purpose is to indicate the Natural Principles governing the relation between Mental Action and Material Conditions... New Age/Psychology Pages 148

Ayesha *by H. Rider Haggard* ISBN: *1-59462-301-3* **$24.95**
Verily and indeed it is the unexpected that happens! Probably if there was one person upon the earth from whom the Editor of this, and of a certain previous history, did not expect to hear again... Classics Pages 380

Ayala's Angel *by Anthony Trollope* ISBN: *1-59462-352-X* **$29.95**
The two girls were both pretty, but Lucy who was twenty-one who supposed to be simple and comparatively unattractive, whereas Ayala was credited, as her Bombwhat romantic name might show, with poetic charm and a taste for romance. Ayala when her father died was nineteen... Fiction Pages 484

The American Commonwealth *by James Bryce* ISBN: *1-59462-286-8* **$34.45**
An interpretation of American democratic political theory. It examines political mechanics and society from the perspective of Scotsman James Bryce Politics Pages 572

Stories of the Pilgrims *by Margaret P. Pumphrey* ISBN: *1-59462-116-0* **$17.95**
This book explores pilgrims religious oppression in England as well as their escape to Holland and eventual crossing to America on the Mayflower, and their early days in New England... History Pages 268

QTY

The Fasting Cure *by Sinclair Upton*   ISBN: *1-59462-222-1* **$13.95**
In the Cosmopolitan Magazine for May, 1910, and in the Contemporary Review (London) for April, 1910, I published an article dealing with my experiences in fasting. I have written a great many magazine articles, but never one which attracted so much attention... New Age/Self Help/Health Pages 164

Hebrew Astrology *by Sepharial*   ISBN: *1-59462-308-2* **$13.45**
In these days of advanced thinking it is a matter of common observation that we have left many of the old landmarks behind and that we are now pressing forward to greater heights and to a wider horizon than that which represented the mind-content of our progenitors... Astrology Pages 144

Thought Vibration or The Law of Attraction in the Thought World   ISBN: *1-59462-127-6* **$12.95**
by William Walker Atkinson   Psychology/Religion Pages 144

Optimism *by Helen Keller*   ISBN: *1-59462-108-X* **$15.95**
Helen Keller was blind, deaf, and mute since 19 months old, yet famously learned how to overcome these handicaps, communicate with the world, and spread her lectures promoting optimism. An inspiring read for everyone... Biographies/Inspirational Pages 84

Sara Crewe *by Frances Burnett*   ISBN: *1-59462-360-0* **$9.45**
In the first place, Miss Minchin lived in London. Her home was a large, dull, tall one, in a large, dull square, where all the houses were alike, and all the sparrows were alike, and where all the door-knockers made the same heavy sound... Childrens/Classic Pages 88

The Autobiography of Benjamin Franklin *by Benjamin Franklin*   ISBN: *1-59462-135-7* **$24.95**
The Autobiography of Benjamin Franklin has probably been more extensively read than any other American historical work, and no other book of its kind has had such ups and downs of fortune. Franklin lived for many years in England, where he was agent... Biographies/History Pages 332

Name	
Email	
Telephone	
Address	
City, State ZIP	

☐ **Credit Card**   ☐ **Check / Money Order**

Credit Card Number	
Expiration Date	
Signature	

Please Mail to: Book Jungle
PO Box 2226
Champaign, IL 61825
or Fax to: 630-214-0564

ORDERING INFORMATION
web*: www.bookjungle.com*
email*: sales@bookjungle.com*
fax*: 630-214-0564*
mail*: Book Jungle PO Box 2226 Champaign, IL 61825*
or PayPal *to sales@bookjungle.com*

Please contact us for bulk discounts

DIRECT-ORDER TERMS

**20% Discount if You Order
Two or More Books**
Free Domestic Shipping!
Accepted: Master Card, Visa,
Discover, American Express

www.ingramcontent.com/pod-product-compliance
Lightning Source LLC
LaVergne TN
LVHW061226060426
835509LV00012B/1445